# Beginning WordPerfect® 5.1

AF771050

# Beginning WordPerfect® 5.1

Fritz H. Grupe
*University of Nevada — Reno*

WCB Wm. C. Brown Publishers

**Book Team**
Editor Kathy Shields
Software Hotline and Developmental Support Technician *Lisa Schonhoff*
Production Coordinator *Deborah Donner*

**Wm. C. Brown Publishers**
President *G. Franklin Lewis*
Vice President, Publisher *George Wm. Bergquist*
Vice President, Publisher *Thomas E. Doran*
Vice President, Operations and Production *Beverly Kolz*
National Sales Manager *Virginia S. Moffat*
Advertising Manager *Ann M. Knepper*
Marketing Manager *Craig S. Marty*
Editor-in-Chief *Edward G. Jaffe*
Managing Editor, Production *Colleen A. Yonda*
Production Editorial Manager *Julie A. Kennedy*
Production Editorial Manager *Ann Fuerste*
Publishing Services Manager *Karen J. Slaght*
Manager of Visuals and Design *Faye M. Shilling*

Cover design by Sailer & Cook Creative Services

WordPerfect ® is a registered trademark of WordPerfect, Inc.

Copyright © 1991 by Wm. C. Brown Publishers. All rights reserved

Library of Congress Catalogue Number: 90-84173

ISBN: 0-697-10791-4

No part of this publication may be reproduced, stored in a retrieval system, or transmitted, in any form or by any means, electronic, mechanical, photocopying, recording or otherwise, without the prior written permission of the publisher.

Printed in the United States of America by Wm. C. Brown Publishers, 2460 Kerper Boulevard, Dubuque, IA 52001

10 9 8 7 6 5 4 3 2 1

# Contents

# Preface

This book has been written to teach its readers to use WordPerfect 5.1 software effectively. It offers practical, hands-on instruction in the use of a highly successful, commercial quality word processing program. This package is widely used in business and education. This software is fully functioned and capable of illustrating most of the major applications that one can develop with other commercial software packages of a similar nature.

Intended to meet several needs, *Beginning WordPerfect 5.1* can be useful in many settings. It can be used as a supplemental laboratory manual for courses that introduce students to computers and their applications, such as Introduction to Computing in Business, Computer Literacy, and Introduction to Microcomputer Software.

This book can also be used as a stand-alone text for short courses that focus on educating students in the main uses of microcomputers. The tutorial orientation of this book allows it to be used by a learner who wishes to work independently. The instructional approach utilized is entirely hands-on and step by step. Exercises are presented with detailed instructions on moving from the identification of a computing problem to its solution.

Each chapter concludes with a group of exercises that reinforce the techniques learned in that chapter. The exercises closely parallel the design of the document, worksheet, or database file presented in the chapter. In some cases, exercises are reused in subsequent chapters to enhance the student's product and to enable students to practice new techniques without unnecessary data entry.

A summary of the complete WordPerfect menu hierarchy is included for instructors who wish to cover material beyond the scope of this book. A glossary of WordPerfect terminology will also be helpful to students.

Much appreciation is due to the following persons who assisted in the development of this book:
**Brent Bowman**, University of Nevada, Reno
**Sharon F. Harvey**, Normandale Community College
**Prasad Kilari**, University of Nevada, Reno
**Mark Simkin**, University of Nevada, Reno

Their assistance and the special assistance given by Arthur Broten and Kerry Chase in the completion of this book is gratefully acknowledged.

# Chapter 1

# An Easy Entry into Word Processing

**Chapter Outline**



WordPerfect is a powerful word processor that can be used to create documents as simple as a one-page letter or as complex as a textbook. It is easy to begin using WordPerfect and, as your requirements grow more complex, you will find that WordPerfect has capabilities to satisfy complicated formatting requirements. In this chapter you will create a very brief business memorandum with few special formatting requirements. In doing so you have the opportunity to

1. Understand how word processors function;
2. Obtain a WordPerfect working disk;
3. Enter text into a document;
4. Move the cursor in small and large steps;
5. Edit and correct text with operations such as insert and delete;
6. View the available Help screens;
7. Print your document;
8. Save and back up your file.

## INTRODUCTION TO WORDPERFECT

Once you have used it, word processing is something you'll never want to do without. How many times have you had to make do with a poorly typed document because you didn't have the energy to retype it? Or have you wanted to redo a term paper because you found typographical errors, strikeovers, misspellings, or missing sentences--yet there wasn't time for another draft? Have you had to retype an entire page of a term paper to leave room for footnotes? Or have you wished that you had the luxury of moving some of the paragraphs and sentences to different places in your paper to give your paper better flow?

These and a hundred other wishes are answered with word processing software like WordPerfect. Word processors enable you to create documents that are stored as files on diskettes. Once created, these documents can be recalled, edited, and printed any number of times. To make changes and to review your revised documents without having to retype them is one of the most useful capabilities of your microcomputer. Among the features that you will appreciate having are:

1. Extensive **Help screens** that are called up quickly to help you if you forget how to complete a command;
2. **WYSIWYG** (What you see is what you get). The monitor screen in front of you can print a document almost exactly as you see it;
3. Extensive **cursor and screen movement capabilities** that allow you to move with speed and accuracy within documents you create;
4. **Function key commands** that are efficient to use;
5. **Editing commands** that allow alteration and revision of text material including moving and duplicating blocks of text, reformatting files, and recalling blocks of text that are deleted in error;
6. **Page and line formatting commands** that help you to design the appearance of printed output with control over the placement of such features as tabs, margins, footnotes, page numbers, headers, and footers;
7. Other **special features**, including global search and replace, the combining of files, the use of alternate font styles such as underlining and boldface, and file merging;
8. **Control over columns**, allowing you to shape text in correct, aesthetically pleasing patterns.

Not all of the diverse features of WordPerfect can be covered in this book, but by working through the exercises and by reading the explanations of how WordPerfect functions you will become proficient in its use. If you wish to go on to more advanced features you will have no difficulty. The WordPerfect Manual describes WordPerfect's advanced capabilities.

### Terminology

Word processing is different from typing in the nicest ways. Although most of the new words and concepts are discussed as they are needed, perhaps a few terms introduced now will be helpful in obtaining a feeling for what word processing software can do that typewriters cannot.

**Word wrap** allows you to type the words of a paragraph without pressing the Enter key. On a typewriter you press the carriage return at the end of every line. In word processing, you simply type and the software determines how many words fit on a line. When the number of words exceeds the line length, the next word is automatically wrapped around to the next line. If you are a good typist, you can continue typing without looking at the screen to see where the margins are.

WordPerfect places a **soft return** at the end of a line when it is using word wrap. A soft return permits easy reformatting if the paragraph is given different margins, or if words are added and deleted, without your having to adjust words. Pressing the Enter key, however, enters a **hard return,** which cannot be reformatted by the word processor.

The **cursor** is the flashing underline that appears in the work area on your screen. The cursor identifies where text is placed if you start typing, or where commands for such actions as deletion or blocking take effect.

Keys **automatically repeat** when they are held down for more than a fraction of a second. WordPerfect is sufficiently fast that you rarely experience "type ahead," in which the remembered keystrokes exceed the typical limit of nineteen used by DOS. If you exceed the limit of remembered strokes, as when you hold down an arrow key too long, WordPerfect beeps at you. The beep does not affect your file. It is a gentle reminder that you are attempting to type characters that the computer cannot retain. When you hear the beep, slow down. Since the computer does not remember more than its limit of keystrokes, in some circumstances it may be necessary to retype some of the keystrokes.

If you reformat a paragraph, or an entire document, with new margins, WordPerfect automatically fills the lines with the greatest number of words possible. If the margins are widened, the number of words on each line is increased. The number is decreased if the margins are narrowed.

Keys are not restricted to typing only one character or carrying out a single function. **Alternate meanings** have been assigned to function keys. These alternate meanings are activated when the keys are pressed at the same time as either the Ctrl, Alt, or Shift keys.

WordPerfect, when it prints the document, produces a straight right-hand margin. This is because it automatically inserts blank spaces in front of some words to place the last printable character next to the right margin. This is called **full justification**. The type of justification can be changed so only the left margin is justified (ragged), so a line is centered, or so only the right margin is justified. WordPerfect can carry out the **automatic hyphenation** of words by breaking them into syllables.

### WordPerfect Operations

There are five kinds of operations that you can conduct with WordPerfect:

1. **File operations** allow you to load, save, or read files on the disk.
2. **Data entry** allows you to enter text and embedded, or invisible, control commands into your document.
3. **Editing** commands change the text on the screen.
4. **Cursor and screen movement** commands change the location of the cursor or alter your view of the text but do not change the text in any way.
5. **Page and line format** changes affect such features as margins and tab stops.

WordPerfect permits operations on blocks of text. When you must work on large blocks of text, for instance, when you wish to move a paragraph from one location to another, you use a process called **blocking.** Pressing the Alt and F4 keys marks the beginning of the block. Moving the cursor to a new location causes the block to be **blocked.** Blocked text has a different appearance from the surrounding text; it appears in reverse video. After the text has been marked, the block operations can be executed. Block operations include moving a block from one location to another, copying (duplicating) the block to another location, saving part of a document into a new file, and deleting a block of text.

## VERSIONS OF WORDPERFECT

WordPerfect is available in several versions. The most recent complete version is numbered 5.1. All of the commands given in this book are built around version 5.1. Most of the commands are similar to those in version 5.0.

## PRINTER SELECTION

It is assumed in this text that you are using a copy of WordPerfect that has been preconfigured for the printer you are using. If you are working in a networked laboratory, WordPerfect should have been preconfigured for the printer you are to use.

In the event that your laboratory uses several printers, you will have to select a printer to print on. The printer selection section of the WordPerfect manual describes this procedure in detail. Review this information if it applies to your situation.

## CREATING FILE DISKETTES

You need a diskette on which to save files. Check the diskettes with the DOS DIR command to be sure that they have been formatted, and that they do not contain any files that you need to save. When you have obtained a diskette that can be used, format it by placing the diskette in drive A. Make sure you are at the C> prompt and enter

| | |
|---|---|
| **format a:** | The format command. You may choose to use FORMAT A: /V to assign a volume name to the disk as well |
| ↵ | Enter key |
| ↵ | Enter key, for no volume label |

When the formatting process is complete, respond N to the prompt asking whether you wish to format another diskette, and place the second diskette in drive A when instructed to do so. Label the first diskette with your name, address, and telephone number, and the phrase *WP-Original Files.* Label the second diskette with the same information about yourself and the phrase *WP-Backup Files.*

## LOADING WORDPERFECT

This text assumes that you are working with a hard disk drive microcomputer. This may not be the case. Consequently, your instructor must inform you about how to access WordPerfect and the other software used in this book if you are using a dual drive or networked floppy disk systems. If WordPerfect has been properly installed, the following procedure enables you to get started:

1. Place the formatted diskette labeled *Original Files* in drive A for saving document files (as opposed to the WordPerfect program).
2. Be sure that your printer and monitor are turned on. Sometimes this is done at the time the computer is turned on, but often they must be switched on separately.
3. The DOS C> prompt should be visible. Before proceeding, check to see what files exist on the diskette in the A drive by typing

   **dir a:**

   This command allows you to see what files may already exist (after you have been creating documents) so that you do not accidentally reuse a filename that is already present. You can also determine that you are using the correct diskette on which to save your files. Assuming that the DOS C> prompt is showing, enter

4. **cd \:wp51**

5. **wp**

6. You then see the blank work screen shown in Figure 1-1.

**Figure 1-1.** WordPerfect Screen

The blinking cursor is in the upper left corner of the screen and a status line will show:

1. The **document number**. WordPerfect allows you to work with two documents concurrently. Normally, you work with only one, so the document number should almost always be **1.** If you see **Doc 2,** return to document 1 by simultaneously pressing Shift and F3.
2. **The cursor location.** The location of the cursor in the file is shown by page (**Pg**), vertical position on the page (**Ln**), and by horizontal position on the page (**Pos**). The (Pos)ition of the cursor is generally at 8 inches or less, since most documents have right margins that must fit on paper 8 1/2 inches wide. It is possible to widen the right margin when wider paper is used. Then the Pos number may well be greater than 8 inches. Pos may be flashing on and off. This indicates that the Num Lock key is on. Remove the flashing by toggling the Num Lock once.
3. From time to time other messages may appear on the left side of the status line.

## A BUSINESS MEMORANDUM

It may come as a surprise, but many important applications for computer usage do not involve mathematical manipulations. Word processing is, perhaps, the most readily identifiable use for a computer. Increasingly, businesses and organizations of all types are using word processing to improve their communications. Word processing is not solely the domain of secretaries. Many professionals spend considerable amounts of their time writing. The first application for which WordPerfect is used here is to create a business memorandum. A memorandum is a useful document to start with because it is not difficult to format. The memorandum in Figure 1-2, for instance, uses block paragraphs (the first line is not indented) and it does not have any underlining, bolding, or special columnar information. Learning to create this memorandum provides you with enough information about word processing to enable you to create many other documents that do not require special features, documents such as letters, class notes, and simple term papers.

## THE CANCEL KEY

The function keys serve a wide variety of purposes, many of which are described in this text. If you press a function key and receive a menu or screen with which you are not familiar, or which should not be present, press the F1 key to cancel the command. Pressing F1, the Cancel key, returns you to the normal WordPerfect entry screen.

## ENTERING TEXT

The cursor is placed at the start of the document. If you are revising a document that already exists, the cursor appears at the same location. The first portion of this exercise is to help you become familiar with text entry. Shown in Figure 1-2 is a memorandum that you are to type as it appears. When creating this memorandum, do not press Enter at the end of most lines. As you type you will notice how WordPerfect wraps the words from one line to the next. You do not have to hit the Enter key. You need only press the Enter key twice after the *Date:*, *To:*, *Fr:*, and *Re:* lines and twice after the last character of the first paragraph.

It is likely that the first line of your first paragraph may wrap to the second line at a point different from the text displayed below, in which case the line endings of your entire paragraph differ from those shown. This is a normal function of your particular system and is not a problem. WordPerfect adjusts the number of characters on a line to match the characteristics of the printer and default font selected for your system. Fonts conventionally chosen for standard text range from ten to fifteen characters per inch. Consequently, the number of characters and words that display on your screen may be different from that shown throughout this text. Simply continue to type in the text and allow the automatic wrap to control the form of your paragraph.

```
Date: September 15, 1991

To: Vice President T. L. White

Fr: Mr. F. Y. Black, Director, Marketing & Sales

Re: Departmental Computer Equipment

It has become increasingly clear that our department can save the
company money in a number of areas if it had immediate access to a
microprocessor.  I will cite three instances in which we could have
doe a better job and have been more productive.  J. Grey produced
a fifty page report for the XYZ Company that had to be retyped 3
times as it was revised and improved.  We needed to produce three
graphic displacys for a presentation to the ABC Corporation and
were told by the Graphics Department that they could not be made
abailable until two weaks after they were needed.  Finally, I had
to produce a projection of our expenditures for the next three year
planning period.  Without access to a spreadsheet accounting
program, this three hour task took a full day.

I believe that the Marketing and Sales Department should be allowed
to acquire a microcomputer with approopriate spreadsheet, graphics
and word processing software.  M. Brown in our department has taken
several computer courses and workshops.  She feels that she can
provide the training required for our staff.  With your approval
and budgetary support, we can help to maintain corporate
profitability.
```

**Figure 1-2.** Sample Memorandum

There are several words that are deliberately misspelled. These errors should be typed as they appear. They will be corrected later. If you make mistakes of your own, don't worry. If you catch a mistake right away, use the Backspace key to erase the character that is to the left and start typing again. If you miss some mistakes, correct them later.

Type in the text from Figure 1-2 and use the Enter key only as noted.

The memorandum's text is entered between a left margin which is indented 1 inch from the edge of the paper and a right margin which is indented 1 inch from the right edge of an 8 1/2 inch by 11 inch sheet of paper. These are the default margin settings. This means that a line of text would take up a maximum of 6 1/2 inches before wrapping to the next line. How many characters actually fit between these margins depends upon the size of the characters (font size) in use. Altering margins is covered in Chapter 5: Advanced WordPerfect Usage.

## CHANGING THE DEFAULT DIRECTORY

When you initially enter the WordPerfect work screen the default directory is C:. This can be changed so all listing, saving, and printing of files is done from a disk other than C:. To change the directory to A:, the one you want to work in, enter

| | |
|---|---|
| **F5** | F5 key, to change the directory. Notice the prompt in the lower line indicating that an equal sign should be typed if you wish to change the default directory. |
| = | Equal sign to change the directory |
| **a:** | A prompt to indicate which directory to change to |
| ◄┘ | Enter key |
| **F1** | F1 key, to return to the work screen. F1 prevents the Directory A:\ screen from appearing. If you do see this screen, press the F7 key to return to the work screen. The default directory is A:. |

## SAVING YOUR FILE

It is a good idea to save your files frequently as you work on them. This protects you if there is a loss of power or if you commit a major error. Also, if you have to exit WordPerfect before you finish with the exercise you have to save your file and return to it later. Save the file by entering

| | |
|---|---|
| **F10** | Function key F10, the Save Files key. The Save Files key saves the file but does not clear the document from the screen. |
| **MEMO** | The name of your file, which can be entered in upper or lowercase |
| ◄┘ | Enter key |

If you plan to continue, do not execute the next six commands. If you must exit WordPerfect now, enter

| | |
|---|---|
| **F7** | Function key F7, the Exit key |
| **Y** | **Y**es, to save the document |
| **MEMO** | The name of your file, which can be entered in upper or lowercase |
| ◄┘ | Enter key |
| **Y** | **Y**es, to save your file (appears only after the first time the file has been saved). Upper or lowercase letters may be typed to select options from all WordPerfect prompts and menus. |
| **Y** | **Y**es, to exit WordPerfect. Do not exit WordPerfect by turning off your computer. By exiting properly, WordPerfect removes certain files from your diskette that are no longer needed. |

To retrieve your file, follow the procedure outlined in Chapter 2: Some Next Steps in Word Processing. Remember: using the F10 key to save a file retains the copy of the document in RAM so you can continue editing. Using the F7 key saves the file and clears the document from memory. Also, remember that a clear screen may be present in a document because a person may enter many hard returns (from pressing the Enter key). Thus, it is possible to retrieve a document into another document if you are not careful.

## MOVING THE CURSOR

Excellent typists make typographical mistakes. Great writers rewrite their work. No matter how careful you are, documents you create need to be reworked. Before you can begin to edit your document, you must be able to move the cursor from one location to another. Do not use the Backspace key to move the cursor because this key erases all letters to the left of the cursor. You do not wish to have to retype large portions of your text simply to correct spelling errors.

WordPerfect provides a variety of commands that move your cursor to different locations without destroying any of the text that has been created. At this point you shall be introduced to seven groups of cursor movement commands. Practice them as they are described.

The arrow keys on the keypad move the cursor one character at a time in the direction that the arrow is pointing.

Pressing the Home key and then pressing the Left Arrow key moves the cursor to the left margin. The first printable character need not necessarily be in the first character position after the left margin since there may be spaces in front of this character.

The End key moves the cursor beyond the last character on a line. This character also may be a blank.

As your document becomes larger, it can no longer be seen on one screen and it is harder to move to specific locations. Several WordPerfect commands are especially helpful in moving between screens and in making bigger jumps from one place to another.

If the cursor is not on the first or last line, you can move the cursor to the top and bottom of the screen by pressing the grey minus and grey plus keys, respectively. If the cursor is on the first or last line of the screen, the pressing of the grey minus or plus sign advances you to the next screen (assuming that you are in a long document that has additional text above or below your current screen).

PgUp takes the cursor to the page before the current page, while PgDn takes the cursor to the following page. This is a short document, so the cursor cannot be moved beyond page 1.

The key sequence Home, Home, and Up Arrow returns the cursor to the top of the file. Home, Home, and Down Arrow moves the cursor to the bottom of the file.

Within a line, too, there are faster cursor movements than the arrow keys alone. Moving one character at a time with the arrow keys is slow. You can move rapidly by holding the Ctrl (Control) key and then pressing the Left Arrow or Right Arrow keys to jump forward and backward word by word. Hold the Control key down then press the selected arrow key. Finally, release the Control key.

Experiment with these movement keys. A summary of the cursor movement commands discussed so far is shown in Figure 1-3. When toggled on, the Num Lock key on the numeric keypad makes cursor movement keys unavailable.

| KEY | ACTION |
|---|---|
| ↑ | Up one character |
| ↓ | Down one character |
| → | Right one character |
| ← | Left one character |
| **Home- ←** | Left margin |
| **End** | End of line |
| **Grey +** | Bottom of screen or bottom of next screen |
| **Grey -** | Top of screen or top of previous screen |
| **PgUp** | Up one page |
| **PgDn** | Down one page |
| **Home,Home, ↑** | Top of file |
| **Home,Home, ↓** | Bottom of file |
| **Control- →** | Right one word |
| **Control- ←** | Left one word |

**Figure 1-3.** Cursor Movement Commands

When you are moving your cursor, try to make your moves as quickly as possible. Much time is wasted by moving one character at a time with the arrow keys when another keystroke combination takes the cursor to its destination more quickly. You will be surprised at how quickly you memorize the keystrokes if you practice them.

The document in Figure 1-4 is short enough that you can see most of it on one screen. Many documents, of course, are not this short. Many of the cursor movement keys move the cursor into those portions of the document that are out of view but are still part of the document.

Date: September 15, 1991

To: ~~Vice President~~ T. L. White

Fr: ~~Mr.~~ F. Y. Black, Director, Marketing & Sales

Re: Departmental Computer Equipment

could<br>
It has become increasingly clear that our department ~~can~~ save the<br>
^<br>
company money in a number of areas if it had immediate access to a<br>
computer 3<br>
micro~~processor~~. I will cite ~~three~~ instances in which we could have<br>
n ^ could ^<br>
doe a better job and have been more productive. J. Grey produced<br>
^ 50- ^<br>
a ~~fifty~~ page report for the XYZ Company that had to be retyped 3<br>
^ 3<br>
times as it was revised and improved. We needed to produce ~~three~~<br>
^<br>
graphic displa~~e~~ys for a presentation to the ABC Corporation and<br>
^<br>
were told by the Graphics Department that they could not be made<br>
v 2 e<br>
a~~b~~ailable until ~~two~~ we~~a~~ks after they were needed. Finally, I had<br>
^ ^ ^ 3-<br>
to produce a projection of our expenditures for the next ~~three~~ year<br>
^<br>
planning period. Without access to a spreadsheet accounting<br>
3-<br>
program, this ~~three~~ hour task took a full day.<br>
^

I believe that the Marketing and Sales Department should be allowed to acquire a microcomputer with appro~~e~~priate spreadsheet, graphics<br>
^<br>
and word processing software. M. Brown in our department has taken several computer courses and workshops. She feels that she can<br>
by<br>
provide the training required ~~for~~ our staff. With your approval<br>
^<br>
and budgetary support, we can ~~help to~~ maintain corporate profitability.

**Figure 1-4.** Document with Editorial Notes

## EDITING

The rewriting of a document involves many kinds of changes. The most obvious changes are the correction of spelling, grammatical, and typographical errors. Other changes may be more significant, including the movement or deletion of large blocks of text. Several editing commands are utilized here and others are introduced later. Assume that you had printed out the memorandum, corrected it by hand, and the changes you wished to make appear in Figure 1-4. What commands help you to make those corrections?

The following instructions guide you through some of the changes outlined in the edited copy. Others you can make on your own after you have been shown the correct technique.

### Deleting Characters

The Del (Delete) key deletes the character immediately above the cursor. Place your cursor under the first o in the misspelled word *approopriate*. Press

**Del** The Delete key. Notice that the *o* was removed and that the rest of the line was pulled left.

The Backspace key deletes the character to the left of the cursor. There is an unneeded *c* in the word *displacys*. Place your cursor under the *y* and press

**Backspace** Backspace key. The letter *c* is erased and that portion of the line to the right of the cursor is pulled over.

### Deleting Words

The words *help to* at the end of the second paragraph are superfluous and should be removed. With the cursor underneath any letter in a word, the simultaneous pressing of the Control and Backspace keys deletes the entire word. Move your cursor under the *h* in *help* and press

**Ctrl-Backspace** Control and Backspace keys pressed simultaneously, to delete *help*. The space following a word is deleted along with the word. Place your cursor under either the *o* or the *t* in *to*.

**Ctrl-Backspace** Control and Backspace, to delete the word *to.*

### The Cancel/Undelete Key

Sometimes you can delete a word, or even a larger block of text, only to find that it really should not have been deleted. When WordPerfect deletes any block of characters, it places a copy of those characters in a portion of RAM where it can be retrieved. Undo the deletion by pressing

**F1** Function key F1, the Cancel/Undelete key, *help to* is reinserted at the location of the cursor. The inserted text is highlighted. This key also cancels commands that are initiated, but not completed. Therefore, it does not reinsert deleted text in the middle of a command sequence, but cancels the command you began.

**1** To restore the previously deleted characters. WordPerfect saves the three most recently deleted character strings. Pressing *2* instead of *1* shows you the previous deletion. You restored *help to,* return the cursor to the word *to* and delete it again with

**Ctrl-Backspace** Control and Backspace, to delete the word

**Inserting Text**

To insert the word *could* between *and* and *have*, place your cursor under the space between the two words and press

| | |
|---|---|
| **Space** | Space bar, to insert one space. Then type |
| **could** | The word to be inserted |

With this insertion the characters on the line are pushed to the right. They may exceed the line length. As additional characters are entered the line is extended. WordPerfect takes care of the reformatting of the paragraph when you move your cursor to a new location and perhaps sooner if you enter many extra characters or if you move the cursor with an arrow key. Reformatting realigns the paragraph within the current margins.

Replace the spelled out numbers with the Arabic numerals. This requires you to delete the words with Control and Backspace keys. Insert the numbers by typing them in. Hyphens should be included in the words *50-page, 3-hour,* and *3-year.*

**Typeover**

The word *microprocessor* is to be replaced by the word *microcomputer.* You do not have to delete an entire word, only to have to retype part of it. There are many ways to approach this change. You can delete part of the word, letter by letter, with the Delete or Backspace keys. You can delete the entire word by pressing Control and Backspace. You can also place the cursor under the *p* and press the Space Bar to make *processor* a separate word and then press Control and Backspace to delete the *processor* portion of the word. Instead, place your cursor under the *p.* Now press

| | |
|---|---|
| **Ins** | Insert key. Observe that the word *Typeover* appears on the status line. Typeover is a mode of typing in which the letters you type replace the letters previously on the line. Then type |
| **computer** | The word to be inserted. This leaves you with the word *microcomputerr* |
| **Del** | Delete key; delete the extra *r* |
| **Ins** | Insert key. The mode of character entry toggles between insertion and typeover each time the Insert key is pressed. The mode you leave WordPerfect in is a matter of choice, although most people prefer the insert mode. |

**Entering Tabs**

The Tab key moves the cursor according to tab settings contained in a tab settings ruler. The default tab settings WordPerfect provides are 1/2 inch apart. Tab keys insert tabs into the document. If pressed many times, the Tab key moves to the last tab setting on a line and stops there. Pressing the Tab key again does not move the cursor to the next line. Indent the first paragraph by moving the cursor beneath the letter *I* in *It* and pressing

**Tab** Tab key, to insert a tab. The line is pushed to the right. When the cursor is moved, the paragraph is rejustified.

If, when the Tab key is pressed, the cursor moves but a tab is not inserted, press the Insert key to change from typeover mode to insert mode.

**Entering and Removing Blank Lines**

If you have extra blank lines in your text, they can be removed in two ways. One way is to place your cursor behind the last letter of the previous line and to press the Delete key. This deletes the hard return at the end of the line, bringing the following line up if words from the line that follows fit. You can also put the cursor on the blank line and use the Backspace key. This also removes the invisible end of line marker to join the two lines. For instance, place your cursor on the blank line between the two paragraphs and enter

| | |
|---|---|
| ◂┘ | Enter key, to add an extra line |
| **Backspace** | Backspace key, to remove the extra line |

Lines of text can be broken by placing your cursor at the point where a break is to occur and pressing the Enter key.
The editing commands introduced thus far are summarized in Figure 1-5.

| KEY | ACTION |
|---|---|
| **Del**(ete) | Delete character above cursor |
| **Backspace** | Delete character to left of cursor |
| **Ctrl-Backspace** | Delete word above cursor |
| **F1** | Reinsert a previous deletion |
| **Ins** | Toggle between insert and typeover |

**Figure 1-5.** Selected Editing Keys

Finish editing the memorandum with these commands. When complete, the memorandum should look like Figure 1-6.

Date: September 15, 1991

To: T. L. White

Fr: F. Y. Black, Director, Marketing and Sales

Re: Departmental Computer Equipment

It has become increasingly clear that our department could save the company money in a number of areas if it had immediate access to a microcomputer. I will cite 3 instances in which we could have done a better job and could have been more productive. J. Grey produced a 50-page report for the XYZ Company that had to be retyped 3 times as it was revised and improved. We needed to produce 3 graphic displays for a presentation to the ABC Corporation and were told by the Graphics Department that they could not be made available until 2 weeks after they were needed. Finally, I had to produce a projection of our expenditures for the next 3-year planning period. Without access to a spreadsheet accounting program, this 3-hour task took a full day.

I believe that the Marketing and Sales Department should be allowed to acquire a microcomputer with appropriate spreadsheet, graphics, and word processing software. M. Brown in our department has taken several computer courses and workshops. She feels that she can provide the training required by our staff. With your approval and budgetary support, we can maintain corporate profitability.

**Figure 1-6.** Completed Memorandum

## USING HELP SCREENS

If you need assistance with some of the commands you may choose while creating, editing, and printing documents, there is a series of useful Help screens you can employ to remind you of the functions of the keys. The educational version of WordPerfect has only one Help screen. Call up Help by pressing

**F3** The Help screen gives you two ways of reaching further Help screens

Pressing an alphabetic character presents a screen with commands that begin with that letter. Pressing a *U*, for example, tells you how to underline and undelete. Pressing the function key with or without pressing the Alt, Ctrl, or Shift keys displays information about the function of the key combination pressed. You are invited to press

↵ Enter key, to exit Help

## SAVING AND BACKING UP YOUR FILE

When your document has been completed, save your file by pressing

**F10** Function key F10, the Save Files key for saving a document. Since the file was saved before, the name of the file, MEMO, appears automatically.

**◂┘** Enter, to save your file

**Y** Yes, to replace the old, uncorrected document with the new, revised version of MEMO

Whenever you are asked to replace a previously existing file, if you answer *Y*, the new file (the one you have been working on) replaces or overwrites the old file. Once overwritten, the old file cannot be recovered. Respond with *N* if you wish to save the old file.

Save your file again on your backup diskette by removing the files diskette from drive A and replacing it with your backup diskette. Save the file to the backup diskette with the same keystrokes.

## PRINTING YOUR FILE

Now that the editing of the memorandum is finished and it has been saved, print out the document. In the next chapter you will revise and add text to the memorandum. To print out the file, check to see that the printer is turned on, displays either *on-line* or *select,* and has paper. Then press

**Shift-F7** Shift and function key F7 pressed together, Print, to obtain the Print menu shown in Figure 1-7.

```
Print

     1 - Full Document
     2 - Page
     3 - Document on Disk
     4 - Control Printer
     5 - Multiple Pages
     6 - View Document
     7 - Initialize Printer

Options

     S - Select Printer                    Epson LQ-500
     B - Binding Offset                    0"
     N - Number of Copies                  1
     U - Multiple Copies Generated by      WordPerfect
     G - Graphics Quality                  Medium
     T - Text Quality                      High



Selection: 0
```

Figure 1-7. Print Menu

| | |
|---|---|
| 1 | Numeral *1* (or *F*) to print the full document |

## EXITING WORDPERFECT

Exit WordPerfect by pressing

| | |
|---|---|
| **F7** | Function key F7, the Exit key. You see the prompt |
| | **Save Document? (Y/N) Yes (No)** |
| **N** | No. Do not save your file again since it was saved just before printing. You see the prompt |
| | **Exit WP? (Y/N) No** |
| **Y** | Yes, to exit WordPerfect. You could respond *N* to clear the screen and to begin typing another document |

In the sequence just described you saved your file first with the F10 key. The F10 key does not exit you from WordPerfect. Then you exited with the F7 key. When you wish to save your file, you may choose to press the F7 key first. Since this key asks you to save your file before exiting, you can avoid using the F10 at all.

## CONFIRMING THE PRESENCE OF THE FILE

When the DOS prompt returns, you can confirm that the file was saved by entering

**dir a:**

to see the response

```
Volume in drive A has no label
Directory of A:\
MEMO         1343 2-15-89 1:07a
  1 File(s)    360448 bytes free
```

You can go on with other computing activities at this point or you can turn the computer off.

## EXERCISES

A. Create the following letter, just as written, with the filename A:PLAINSMN. Bear in mind that the wrapped lines of your text may prove to be of different length than shown here.

```
May 19, 1990

Charles D. May
Editor, Daily Plainsman
Mountsville, IA 97673

Dear Mr. May:

I am a freshman at the state university this yaer. My major is
journalizm. Professor Margaret Scotte who was a teacher of yours
suggested that I contact you about the possibility of obtaing a
summer job with your newspaper.

Thus far, I have taken two English composition courses and Jour.
200, Newspaper Writing. I especially ejnoy preparing human
interest articles. Three of my class assignments have been
published in our school newspaper. Dr. Scotte said that she would
be happy to be a reference for me if you wished to contact her.

Iwill retrun to Mountsville for summer vacation on June 2nd. I
will contact you then to see if any opening exist.

Sincerely,

Milton Morehoutte
Box 123,
Duffy Dormitory
State University
Anytown, IA 97621
```

After you have created the file, print it. Then make the following changes:

1. Insert
   --a blank space between *I* and *will* on the first line of the third paragraph,
   --*in* in the word *obtaing,*
   --the sentence, *I received an A in all three courses.* after sentence 1 of paragraph 2,
   --the sentence, *I will be available from June 2 to Sept. 3.* between the two sentences in paragraph 3,
   --the student's telephone number *(303-566-7899)* after his address,
   --an *s* after *opening,* in the last paragraph,
   --a comma before and after the phrase, *who was a teacher of yours*.
2. Replace
   --the lowercase *s* and *u* in *state university* with uppercase letters,
   --the *z* with an *s* in *journalizm*,
   --the words *your newspaper* in the last line of the first paragraph with *the Daily Plainsman*,
   --the word *happy* with *pleased.*
3. Separate the sentence beginning, *Dr. Scotte said . . .* into a separate paragraph by inserting a hard return.
4. Insert tabs at the beginning of each paragraph.
5. Fix any remaining errors in the document.

B. Create the following letter with the filename A:JOHNSON as it is written:

February 19, 1991

Jack Johnson
Acme Campers and Trailers
270 East Market Street
Warbuck, CA 27779

Dear Mr. Warbuck:

This letter is to advice you that Ms. Marsha Dean who has been your acount representative for the last four years hsa been promoted to the position of Vice President for Design and Production. In her new position, Ms. Dean will be able to apply the knowledge about the recreational vehicle retail sales market to the introduction of a new product line. The phaeton line of camper tops to be announced shrotly will be trend setters for sure.

Mr. Hugh Falkner will be assigned to service your account as of June 21, 1987. Mr. Falkner has been with the company for six years and has a through knowledge of the campout products line of camper tops and trailers. He has owned his own camping supplies company, so I am sure that he will be able to solve you problems.

Pleaselet us know if their is any way by which we can sevre you better.

Sincerely,

Mary Muldowner,
Pressident,
Campout Products

After you have created the file, print it. Then make the following changes:

1. Insert
   --a blank space between *Please* and *let* in the last sentence,
   --the second *c* in the word *acount*,
   --the sentence *Mr. Falkner can be reached at 205-566-7672.* after the single sentence in paragraph 3,
   --the phrase, *I am pleased to announce that* as an introduction to the first sentence in paragraph 2,
   --an *o* in the word *through* to make it *thorough*,
   --an *r* after *you* in *you problems*,
   --the word *quickly* before the period, but after the word *problems*.

2. Replace
   - --the lowercase *c* and *p* in *campout products* with uppercase letters,
   - --the *c* with an *s* in *advice*,
   - --the lowercase *p* in *phaeton* with an uppercase *P*,
   - --*their* with *there* in the last sentence,
   - --the word *sure* at the end of paragraph 1 with *certain*,
   - --the spelling of the name *Falkner* with the spelling *Faulkner* throughout.
3. Delete
   - --the extra *s* in *Pressident*,
   - --the phrase *line of* in the second paragraph (and add an apostrophe to the end of *Products*).
4. Insert tab markers at the beginning of each paragraph.
5. Fix any remaining errors in the document.

C. Create another memorandum for Mr. Black in which progress in a new sales campaign is reported to the president of XYZ Corporation.

D. Write a letter home carefully explaining to your parents how the costs at college have risen dramatically and asking for money.

E. Begin writing your next term paper with WordPerfect.

F. Prepare a one-page biographical sketch of yourself.

# Chapter 2

# Some Next Steps in Word Processing

**Chapter Outline**

Retrieving a File
Editing Text
Tabs and Rulers
Using Special Fonts
    Underlining
    Bolding
Reveal Codes
Searching
    Forward Search
    Reverse Search
    Finding Words
File Copies Versus File Originals
Saving Under a New Filename
Backing Up Your File
Printing
Searching and Replacing
    Replacement with Confirmation
    Cancel Command
    Replacement without Confirmation
Quitting without Saving Your File
Exercises

It is a rare document that can be created and printed without revision. The memorandum created in the last chapter was short and simple. It could have been written in one session by a person familiar with word processing. Often, however, a document is typed by one person and edited by another. Revisions made by the editor might be made in the file by still another person. This chapter extends your knowledge of WordPerfect by showing you how to:

1. Retrieve a previously created file;
2. Add text to that file;
3. Use the search and the search-and-replace commands;
4. Use boldfacing and underlining fonts;
5. Modify the margins and tabs for your document.

## RETRIEVING A FILE

To retrieve your memorandum, boot your computer or, if it is already running, obtain the C> prompt. Place your files diskette in drive A. Then enter

| | |
|---|---|
| cd wp\ | To change the default directory to the directory holding WordPerfect |
| wp | To load WordPerfect from the hard drive. Use the F7 (Exit key) to clear the screen if necessary. To bring your file MEMO into WordPerfect, make sure that the work screen is clear. |
| F5 | Function key F5, the List Files key |
| = | Equal sign, to change the default directory |
| a: | To change the default directory to drive A |
| ↵ | Enter key, to accept A:*.* as the default drive and directory from which to list files |
| ↵ | Enter key, to see the names of the files on the default drive and directory |
| →,←,↑,↓ | Arrow keys, as necessary, to highlight the filename MEMO and to see the List Files screen that looks similar to Figure 2-1. |
| 1 | To retrieve your file and place the cursor at the top of the document. The file should be identical to the file that you saved and printed out in Chapter 1: An Easy Entry into Word Processing. You are ready to alter the document. |

```
03-03-90  01:54p              Directory A:\*.*
Document size:         0   Free:    320,512 Used:       1,618     Files:         1

 .    Current    <Dir>                    | ..    Parent     <Dir>
 WP2-4    .      1,618  03-03-90 01:38p



1 Retrieve; 2 Delete; 3 Move/Rename; 4 Print; 5 Short/Long Display;
6 Look; 7 Other Directory; 8 Copy; 9 Find; N Name Search: 6
```

**Figure 2-1.** The List Files Screen

This procedure is useful when you are not sure of the filename of a document that you wish to retrieve. Sometimes when you do know the filename, it is faster to press Shift and F10 simultaneously. You are prompted for the name of the file you wish to retrieve. If necessary, you can expand the filename by including a directory and pathname.

The List Files screen has many uses in addition to retrieving files. By highlighting a file's name you can:

1. Delete a file from your disk,

2. Rename a file or move it to a different disk or directory if you are using directories,
3. Print a file from disk without accessing the Control Printer options,
4. Look inside a file without retrieving it in order to see whether its contents are what you expected,
5. Change directories if you are using directories,
6. Copy a file to another disk,
7. Reduce the listing of filenames to only those files that contain a target word,
8. Locate a file in the listing by typing its name letter by letter until WordPerfect highlights the filename you desire.

Mr. Black has decided to have his document edited to look as it does in Figure 2-2.

**EDITING TEXT**

The sentence added between paragraphs is to be entered now. Underlines will be added later. Using the cursor movement keys noted in the last chapter, move your cursor to the blank line currently separating the two paragraphs. Enter

| | |
|---|---|
| ◄┘ | Enter key, to enter another blank line above the cursor |
| **Tab** | Tab key, to indent the first word. Then type: |

**This is the only department that does not have a microcomputer for word and data processing operations.**

| | |
|---|---|
| ◄┘ | Enter key, to introduce another blank line |

Practice using the cursor movement commands listed in Figure 1-3. After a short while, believe it or not, the commands begin to come to you with no more thought than it takes to press alphabetic character keys.

Now move to the last character of the last paragraph.

| | |
|---|---|
| **Home,Home,↓** | Home key pressed twice, followed by Down arrow, to move to the last sentence |

Now press

| | |
|---|---|
| ◄┘ | Enter key twice, to end the paragraph and to insert a blank line between it and the paragraph being added |
| **Tab** | Tab key, to indent the next paragraph |

**An assessment of the needs of our department completed by M. Brown has determined that we need a system with these components:**

| | |
|---|---|
| ◄┘ | Enter key. Do not put in the blank line now. |

Date: September 15, 1991

To: T. L. White

Fr: F. Y. Black, Director, Marketing and Sales

Re: Departmental Computer Equipment

It has become increasingly clear that our department could save the company money in a number of areas if it had immediate access to a microcomputer. I will cite 3 instances in which we could have done a better job and could have been more productive. J. Grey produced a 50-page report for the XYZ Company that had to be retyped 3 times as it was revised and improved. We needed to produce 3 graphic displays for a presentation to the ABC Corporation and were told by the Graphics Department that they could not be made available until 2 weeks after they were needed. Finally, I had to produce a projection of our expenditures for the next 3-year planning period. Without access to a spreadsheet accounting program, this 3-hour task took a full day.

This is the only department that does not have a microcomputer for word and data processing operations.

I believe that the Marketing and Sales Department should be allowed to acquire a microcomputer with appropriate spreadsheet, graphics, and word processing software. M. Brown in our department has taken several computer courses and workshops. She feels that she can provide the training required by our staff. With your approval and budgetary support, we can maintain corporate profitability.

An assessment of the needs of our department completed by M. Brown has determined that we need a system with these components:

| | |
|---|---|
| Personal computer, 640KB, hard drive | $2,000.00 |
| Laser printer | 1,500.00 |
| Plotter | 2,000.00 |
| Software | 1,500.00 |
| Computer Furniture | 675.00 |
| Supplies, cables, power protector | 950.00 |
| TOTAL | $8,625.00 |

I shall set up an appointment with you for next week to discuss our request.

**Figure 2-2.**

## TABS AND RULERS

You have already used the Tab key to indent paragraphs. WordPerfect has default tab settings (settings which it uses if you don't deliberately use different settings) which are currently hidden from view. To enter the list of equipment to be purchased and the prices for that equipment, it is awkward to have to keep tabbing. Setting a simpler tab settings ruler would be more efficient. It would also be helpful if the numbers being typed were automatically lined up on the decimal point. To see and to change the current settings in use, press

**Shift-F8** Shift pressed simultaneously with function key F8, the Format key, to see the Format menu, which displays the options for setting Line, Page, Document, and Other formatting options shown in Figure 2-3.

```
Format

     1 - Line
              Hyphenation                       Line Spacing
              Justification                     Margins Left/Right
              Line Height                       Tab Set
              Line Numbering                    Widow/Orphan Protection

     2 - Page
              Center Page (top to bottom)       Page Numbering
              Force Odd/Even Page               Paper Size/Type
              Headers and Footers               Suppress
              Margins Top/Bottom

     3 - Document
              Display Pitch                     Redline Method
              Initial Codes/Font                Summary

     4 - Other
              Advance                           Overstrike
              Conditional End of Page           Printer Functions
              Decimal Characters                Underline Spaces/Tabs
              Language

Selection: 0
```

**Figure 2-3.** Format Screen

**1** Numeral *1* (or *L*) to see the Line Format menu shown in Figure 2-4

```
Format: Line

     1 - Hyphenation                        No

     2 - Hyphenation Zone - Left            10%
                            Right           4%

     3 - Justification                      Full

     4 - Line Height                        Auto

     5 - Line Numbering                     No

     6 - Line Spacing                       1

     7 - Margins - Left                     1"
                   Right                    1"

     8 - Tab Set                            Rel: -1", every 0.5"

     9 - Widow/Orphan Protection            No


Selection: 0
```

Figure 2-4. Line Format Screen

8 To display the current tab settings. The ruler looks like that shown in Figure 2-5a.

```
L....L....L....L....L....L....L....L....L....L....L....L....L....L....L....L...
|    ^    |    ^    |    ^    |    ^    |    ^    |    ^    |    ^    |    ^
0"        +1"       +2"       +3"       +4"       +5"       +6"       +7"
Delete EOL (clear tabs); Enter Number (set tab); Del (clear tab);
Type: Left; Center; Right; Decimal; .= Dot Leader; Press Exit when done.
```

Figure 2-5a. Tab Setting Prompt

Tab markers are, by default, preset at every 1/2 inch and displayed as *L*s. On the second line vertical markers (|) indicate full inch increments and carets (^) designate half-inch increments. Numbers on the next line indicate the relative distance a point is from the current left margin. The numbering begins with 0 inch. If you press and hold down the Left arrow key, the positions from minus one inch to zero inch show also. Within a document, pressing the Tab key moves the cursor from tab setting to tab setting. If the cursor is at the last tab marker on a line, pressing the Tab key does not move the cursor.

There are seven types of tab settings. The *L* setting left-justifies text that is typed after the Tab key is struck. A *C* centers the text on either side of the tab. An *R* right-justifies, or inserts text to the left of the tab. Entering a *D* for a decimal tab justifies the numbers on the decimal point contained in the numbers typed. Typing the period option before typing the *R*, *L*, or *D* causes WordPerfect to insert dots up to the tabbed text, rather than blanks. Look at exercises C, D, and E at the end of this chapter to see how these tab settings function.

To remove a tab, move the cursor to that tab marker with the arrow keys and press the Delete key. All tabs from the location of the cursor to the right can be deleted by entering Control-End. Tabs can be added either by entering the position in tenths of an inch (for instance 1.4 for a tab marker at the fourth period after 1 inch) where the tab is to appear and pressing the Enter key, or by moving the cursor to the correct location and typing the tab letter. Using these adjustment commands, alter the settings to look like those shown in Figure 2-5b.

```
L.................................................D....L....L....L.............
!    ^    !    ^    !    ^    !    ^    !    ^    !    ^    !    ^    !    ^
0"        +1"       +2"       +3"       +4"       +5"       +6"       +7"
Delete EOL (clear tabs); Enter Number (set tab); Del (clear tab);
Type; Left; Center; Right; Decimal; .= Dot Leader; Press Exit when done.
```

**Figure 2-5b.** Revised Tab Settings

Save the setting by pressing

| | |
|---|---|
| **F7** | Function key F7, the Exit key, to exit the tab setting menu |
| ◄┘ | Enter key, to exit the Line Format menu |
| ◄┘ | Enter key, to exit the Format menu |

When you press the Tab key, the cursor moves to the next L-marked tab setting and a tab code is inserted in the document. Any characters you type in after the Tab key appear after the tab marker.

The ruler you created affects the formatting of all the text inserted below the insertion of these settings into the document. It has no effect on those portions of the document which appear above the inserted tab ruler code. Similarly, any code entered is entered at the location of the cursor and affects all text from that point on. Sometimes a code does not appear to have an effect because another code is to the right or below that code, thereby canceling the effect of the first code. Press

| | |
|---|---|
| ◄┘ | Enter key, to insert another blank line |
| **Tab** | Tab key, to insert a tab and to move the cursor to the tab marker |
| **Personal computer, 640KB, hard drive** | The item recommended for purchase |
| **Tab** | Tab key. Notice the prompt "Align char = ." that shows that the decimal point is used to align the numbers. |
| **$2,000.00** | The cost of the computer |
| ◄┘ | Enter key, to start a new line |

Enter the remaining computer components and their prices as they appear in Figure 2-2 by pressing the Tab key, typing the item name, pressing Tab again, typing the cost for the item, and pressing the Enter key. Notice how the numbers align themselves when you press the period. Repeat this sequence until the list is finished.

Enter the final sentence.

## USING SPECIAL FONTS

### Underlining

Two sections of the text in the memorandum are to be underlined. WordPerfect enhances the impact of your writing with these styles of printer output called fonts. One method of including special fonts is to block the text to be underlined. Place the cursor under the *o* in *our* in paragraph 1 and press

| | |
|---|---|
| **Alt-F4** | The Block key, to mark the beginning of the block. Notice the flashing prompt "Block on." |
| **Ctrl→** | Seven Control-Right Arrow key combinations, to highlight seven words and the trailing blank space |
| ← | Left Arrow, to remove the blank space from the block |
| **F8** | The Underline key. The appearance of the letters on the screen change to reflect the use of the underline font and the block highlighting is removed. |

Place your cursor under the *T* in *This* at the beginning of the second paragraph and type

| | |
|---|---|
| **Alt-F4** | The Block key, to mark the beginning of the block |
| ↓ | Down Arrow, to highlight the entire first line |
| **End** | To highlight the entire second line |
| **F8** | The Underline key. After the blocked text is underlined, the blocking is removed. |

### Bolding

The F6 key is the Bold key. It can be employed in the same way as the Underline key. The F6 and F8 keys can be used together to both bold and underline text.

In the two examples used in the memorandum, underlining was introduced after the text was typed. The underlining was applied to a highlighted block. Underlining and bolding can be started during the entry of text. As you are typing, press the appropriate function key or keys (F6 or F8), and continue typing. When you wish to return to normal type, press the same function key(s) to return to normal type.

You can make the same font changes plus numerous others involving the size and appearance of text by using the Font key (Ctrl-F8). In the case of bolding and underlining as here, the effect is the same in one less keystroke by applying the techniques completed above. In a later chapter, however, the Font key is shown to be helpful for managing other kinds of font changes.

## REVEAL CODES

You can usually tell when text has been bolded, underlined, centered, or otherwise altered in appearance by some code that has been inserted. What happens if you decide to change some of these codes? How do you find them? The Alt-F3 key is called the Reveal Codes key. By pressing this key combination you can open a window that lets you see the text and any codes that have been entered. Place your cursor under the first character of the third paragraph and press

| | |
|---|---|
| **Alt-F3** | Alternate and function key F3 pressed simultaneously, the Reveal Codes key, to open a window that, in part, shows, |

```
     I believe that the Marketing and Sales Department should be
C:\WP51\WPFIGS\WP3-2                            Doc 1 Pg 1 Ln 5" Pos 1.5"
{    ▲    ▲    ▲    ▲    ▲    ▲    ▲    ▲    ▲    ▲    ▲    ▲    }    ▲    ▲
[Tab][UND]This is the only department that does not have a microcomputer[SRt]
for word and data processing operations.[und][HRt]
[HRt]
[Tab]I believe that the Marketing and Sales Department should be[SRt]
```

**Figure 2-6.** Reveal Codes

The left brace shows where the left margin is located and the triangles show where the tabs are set for this block of text. **[UND]** is the code for begin underlining. **[und]** closes the underlining. **[Tab]** shows where the tab was inserted by pressing the Tab key. The cursor, located on the **[UND]** code, can be moved with the arrow keys and with any other keystrokes that normally move the cursor. **[SRt]** represents a soft return entered by WordPerfect and **[Hrt]** represents a hard return entered by pressing the Enter key. You can type characters and in fact use virtually all of WordPerfect's features in the Reveal Codes mode. The Delete and Backspace keys can be used to delete characters and codes at the cursor and to the left of the cursor, respectively. Delete any codes that are on your screen that do not appear in the sample shown above. To remove the Reveal Codes window, press

**Alt-F3** The Reveal Codes key, to remove the window

## SEARCHING

### Forward Search

Often, changes to be made in a document are far apart. Visually searching for an incorrectly spelled word or for a phrase can be tedious. You can move directly to a specific word or string of characters with the WordPerfect search command.

Move to the top of the file with the Home, Home, Up Arrow key combination. Suppose that you wished to move to the word *clear* on the first line of the first paragraph. If you press F2 you receive the prompt,

**-> Srch:**

The arrow indicates that the search is to be started from the location of the cursor and proceeds to the end of the document. You do not have to be at the top of the document, but the search stops at the bottom of the document. Thus, a search may not find a character string you are looking for if it is located above the cursor. The cursor is requesting the entry of a string of (one or more) characters you wish to search for. Type

**F2** The Search key
**clear** The word to be searched for
**F2** The Forward Search key, or the Escape key, to begin the search. Pressing this key advances you to the first occurrence of the word being searched for. The cursor stops at the last letter of the search string.

Press F2 twice more. WordPerfect uses *clear* as the default search string because it was the last string of characters searched for. Since this is the only occurrence of the word *clear,* you receive a message

*** Not Found ***

Repeat the search process with a different character string. Return the cursor to the top of the document and type

| | |
|---|---|
| **F2** | The Forward Search key |
| **the** | The word to be searched for; *the* replaces *clear* |
| **F2** | To begin the search |

Continue locating the string *the* by pressing pairs of F2 keys. After the fifth search, however, you find the character string *the*, but the entire word is actually *they*. WordPerfect located the character string *the*, not the word *the*. Because WordPerfect finds the precise string of characters you type, it could find *the* in *other*, *either*, or many other words. The shorter or more common the search string is, the more likely it is that WordPerfect will find many words in addition to the word you are actually seeking.

**Reverse Search**

You can use the simultaneous pressing of the Shift and F2 keys to reverse the direction of the search. The arrow in the prompt shows the direction of the search. Press

| | |
|---|---|
| **Shift-F2** | The Reverse Search key |
| **F2** | To start the search |

Press this key combination until there are no more occurrences of *the* to be found.

**Finding Words**

Return to the top of the document (Home, Home, Up Arrow), then press the F2 key to do a forward search. This time type a blank space with the space bar before and after the characters *the* so that the prompt line reads

**-> Srch:  the**   The word *the* preceded and followed by spaces
^ ^

This defines the word more accurately. The space in front prevents WordPerfect from finding *the* in such words as *bathe* or *lathe* since a blank does not match any other character. The space behind prevents WordPerfect from finding the search string in words such as *they* or *these.* Press the F2 key until the last *the* is found to confirm that WordPerfect finds only *the* as a word.

Three helpful strategies for searching for a word without having to locate intermediate occurrences of the same search string are:

1. Include the spaces on either side of the word to avoid finding the string being sought inside of other words.
2. Don't search for a common word, but search for an uncommon word in the same line. For instance, if you wished to change *the aliens* to *those aliens* don't search for *the*, search for *aliens.*
3. Search for more than one word. The search string can be *the XYZ,* which occurs much less frequently than the word *the* alone.

## FILE COPIES VERSUS FILE ORIGINALS

When you retrieved a file, such as MEMO in this chapter, WordPerfect created a copy of the file on the diskette in RAM. As you make changes to the document you see on the screen, you are changing the copy, not the original. This has several important implications.

First, the good news. You may intentionally retrieve a file and not intend to save it. Suppose you submitted a magazine article for publication and you decided that the file could, with editing, make a chapter in a book you were starting. You don't want to change the original, but neither do you want to have to retype it just to have a different filename. You should retrieve the file as usual, make the changes, but save the file under a new name to protect the original file and to avoid extensive retyping.

More good news. You may execute a command that has widespread and deleterious results. It may be too time-consuming to undo the changes already made. For instance, you may have deleted the word *the* throughout a one hundred-page document. If you don't save the corrupted file, the original is still there. Discard the corrupted file and start over with the original.

Now the bad news. If your computer loses power or if you turn it off before you have saved your document, the changes are lost. Save files regularly! If you make a disastrous mistake, you can return to a relatively current original. If the file is not saved periodically, you may have to make the changes again.

## SAVING UNDER A NEW FILENAME

Normally, when you edit a file you save the file under its original name. However, you may sometimes wish to save the file under a different name. By changing the name a new file is created, and the file with the filename used originally is left unchanged. The memorandum that has been edited and improved can, for instance, be saved as MEMO2, leaving the file MEMO unaltered. Do this by pressing

| | |
|---|---|
| **F10** | The Save File key, to display the prompt |
| | **Document to be saved: A:\MEMO** |
| **MEMO2** | The new name for the file |
| ◄┘ | Enter key, to complete the renaming procedure |

No confirmation command is requested since this is the first time that the file is being saved as MEMO2. Confirmation is only requested when the filename exists already and WordPerfect seeks to avoid the unnecessary altering of a file that should be left intact.

## BACKING UP YOUR FILE

Back up the file by replacing the diskette in drive A with your backup files diskette and entering

| | |
|---|---|
| **F10** | The key for saving a document |
| ◄┘ | Enter key. The remembered filename, MEMO2, is used again. |

## PRINTING

This file is complete. To print out the file, type

Shift-F7 The Print key, to display the Print menu

```
Print

     1 - Full Document
     2 - Page
     3 - Document on Disk
     4 - Control Printer
     5 - Multiple Pages
     6 - View Document
     7 - Initialize Printer


Options

     S - Select Printer                    Epson LQ-500
     B - Binding Offset                    0"
     N - Number of Copies                  1
     U - Multiple Copies Generated by      WordPerfect
     G - Graphics Quality                  Medium
     T - Text Quality                      High




Selection: 0
```

Figure 2-7. The Print Menu

1 To print the document

## SEARCHING AND REPLACING

The previously described search procedure is useful for changing one occurrence of a word. Frequently, there is a need to change many occurrences of a word or phrase. For example, it may not be until after a paper has been completed that it is found that key board should be keyboard or that back space should be backspace. The search-and-replace command makes the desired changes throughout the file where these corrections are to be made. There are two variations on the search-and-replace technique. Both variations begin with pressing the Alt and F2 keys.

You will be making many changes to the memorandum that you have created. The file will not be saved after the changes have been made. Do not worry, for the changes which you are making for illustrative purposes will not damage the properly constructed memorandum, MEMO2.

### Replacement with Confirmation

There are three occurrences of the phrase *our department* in the memorandum. Suppose that Mr. Black decided that this phrase should be changed to read *the Marketing and Sales Department.* In a short memorandum like this, visually locating and exchanging the two phrases would not be difficult. It would be difficult if the file were twenty pages long and contained fifteen instances of the phrase.

Press the Home, Home, and Up Arrow keys to move to the top of the file. To have WordPerfect make the changes throughout the document, press

| | |
|---|---|
| **Alt-F2** | The Search-and-Replace key. You receive the prompt |
| | **w/Confirm? No (Yes)** |
| **Y** | Yes, to indicate that you wish to see each string before the replacement operation is carried out |
| **our department** | The new search string. WordPerfect remembers the previous search string which is replaced by *our department.* |
| **F2** | Function key F2, to enter the search string |
| **the Marketing and Sales Department** | The replacement string |
| **F2** | Function key F2, to enter the replacement string. WordPerfect finds the first occurrence of the string *our department*, and prompts you with |
| | **Confirm? No (Yes)** |
| **Y** | Yes, replace the string. WordPerfect makes the change and continues by locating the next occurrence of *our department.* |
| **N** | No, do not replace the second occurrence of the string (to demonstrate that you have the option of making the change if you wish). The search continues. |
| **Y** | Yes, replace the third occurrence of the string. Wait for the *** Please Wait *** message to disappear before proceeding. |

Each time a *Y* or an *N* is pressed WordPerfect makes a change, if called for, and locates the next occurrence of the search string. If you do not wish the replacement to occur, press *N* and the phrase remains as it was.

Try the search-and-replace operation again. Press the Home, Home, Up Arrow key combination to go to the top of the file. Press

| | |
|---|---|
| **Alt-F2** | The Search and Replace key, to start the search-and-replace operation |
| **Y** | To request that each change be confirmed first |
| **produc** | Search for the string, *produc.* The search string finds *produce, produced,* and *productive* |
| **F2** | Function key F2 |
| **creat** | The replacement string |
| **F2** | Function key F2 |
| **N** | No, do not make the replacement since the word would become *creattive.* (Do you see why?) |

Continue the process of alternately replacing and not replacing the character strings until the last instance of *produc* has been located and changed.

**Cancel Command**

You can terminate the search-and-replace operation at any time by pressing the F1, or Cancel, key. The F1 key cancels nearly every operation that has been started in WordPerfect, not just the search-and-replace operation.

**Replacement without Confirmation**

The ability to see each location of the search string is useful, but you may wish to be able to effect all changes immediately and without individual prompts. There are four occurrences of *we.* Exchange the string *the Marketing and Sales Department* for *we* in one operation by pressing

**Alt-F2** To search and replace. You receive the prompt

**w/Confirm?** No (Yes)

**N** No, or press Enter key, to indicate that you do not wish to see each string before the replacement operation is carried out

**we** The new search string. Note the spaces on either side of the word, *we*.
^ ^ WordPerfect remembers the previous search string, *produc*

**F2** Function key F2, to enter the search string

**the Marketing and Sales Department**
The replacement string, with spaces on both sides of the replacement string

You must include the spaces in front of *the* and after *Department,* since the opening and closing were included in the search string. If you do not include the spaces here, the opening and closing words are united with the words on both sides of the search string.

**F2** Function key F2, to enter the replacement string. WordPerfect finds all occurrences of the string we and makes changes wherever possible, including the *we* in *week* and *were* if you did not put spaces around *we.*

This process is often referred to as a global replacement. Figure 2-8 identifies the search and replace options.

| KEY(S) | ACTION |
|---|---|
| F2 | Search |
| Alt-F2 | Search and Replace |
| Shift-F2 | Reverse Search |
| F1 | Cancel/Undelete |

**Figure 2-8.** Search and Replace Options

## QUITTING WITHOUT SAVING YOUR FILE

You have made several changes to your memorandum. It is not uncommon that global changes create more difficulties than they solve. If that happens, as is the case now, you should not save the corrupted file as MEMO2 because the altered document replaces the good version that was saved just before the printing operation. Press

| | |
|---|---|
| **F7** | The Exit key |
| **N** | **N**o, do not save the file |
| **Y** | **Y**es, exit WordPerfect |

The prompt for DOS appears quickly, and the disk drive light does not go on. These are two indications that the corrupted file was not written to disk.

## EXERCISES

A. Retrieve the letter, PLAINSMN, and
--underline the name of the newspaper, *Daily Plainsman*,
--search for every occurrence of the letters *ou*,
Save the file and then,
--replace every instance of *ti* with *xx*,
--replace every other instance of *al* with *qq*,
--quit without replacing the good version of PLAINSMN with this corrupted version.

B. Retrieve the letter, JOHNSON, and
--use the F6 key to make bold the first appearances of the names, *Ms. Marsha Dean,* and *Mr. Hugh Faulkner,*
--underline the phrase, *solve your problems quickly.*
Save the file and then,
--search for all instances of the word *the*,
--search for all instances of the character string, *the,*
--change all instances of *am* to *xx,*
--change every other instance of *ou* to *in,*
--quit without replacing the good version of JOHNSON with this corrupted version.

C. Create a tab settings ruler that uses Left (L), Right (R), and Decimal (D) tab markers to set up a table as follows:

| **Item** | **Number** | **Amount** |
|---|---:|---:|
| Pencils | 127 | 44.45 |
| Pens | 89 | 114.81 |
| Banners | 20 | 119.00 |
| Pads | 230 | 181.70 |
| Note Books | 75 | 446.25 |
| Paper Packets | 1250 | 2362.50 |
| Total | | 3268.71 |

D. Create a tab settings ruler that uses Left (L), Center (C), and Decimal (D) tabs to set up a table as follows:

| **Company** | **Sales Person** | **Amount** |
|---|---|---|
| ABC Company | Shaw | 192.15 |
| Real Thing Graphics | Wells | 2683.20 |
| Tinker & Tailor | Brownley | 4780.00 |
| Marjoram & Basil, Inc. | Wells | 16.50 |
| Pragmatic Exercise Inc. | Doe | 165.78 |
| Mallory & Mallory | Shaw | 232.33 |

E. Create a tab settings ruler that uses Left (L) and Dotted Left (period, L) tabs to produce part of a table of contents as follows:

```
I.
INTRODUCTION TO COMPUTERS                                      Pg
A Short History of Computers . . . . . . . . . . . . . . . . .  1
Computers in Society . . . . . . . . . . . . . . . . . . . . .  6
The Computer Market . . . . . . . . . . . . . . . . . . . . . . 10
You and the Computer  . . . . . . . . . . . . . . . . . . . . . 16

II.
WORD PROCESSING
What Is Word Processing?  . . . . . . . . . . . . . . . . . . . 17
Introductory Concepts . . . . . . . . . . . . . . . . . . . . . 20
```

WordPerfect has another, more flexible approach to creating tables of contents that is especially useful for long documents that change frequently. Check the WordPerfect Manual for information about this feature.

# Chapter 3

# Word Processing: A Résumé

**Chapter Outline**



The next document you create will be a résumé that requires the use of additional features of WordPerfect. In this chapter you will:

1. Use stored format settings that help you to prepare résumés;
2. Insert font changes as you enter text;
3. Center individual lines and blocks of text between page margins;
4. Move and delete blocks of text;
5. Change uppercase letters to lowercase and vice versa.

Résumés are important documents for individuals since they are often a key component of the applicant screening process used by employers. Résumés are intended to provide up-to-date information about candidates. Consequently, résumés change each time the person's background changes, a condition that encourages the use of a word processor. The structure of a résumé is quite different from many other documents. This structure requires the use of different tab settings than you might use for a memorandum or a book. The résumé you create now will be modified significantly to illustrate how major changes can be made in a document.

Figure 3-1 is a résumé which a student believes will be helpful in applying for jobs after graduation.

**HARRIET HARTLEY**

22 Elm Street
West Washington, NV 89888
707-555-5665

| | |
|---|---|
| **PROFESSIONAL GOAL:** | To work within a challenging company and to interact with the public in a problem-solving environment. |
| **EDUCATION:** | **WEST WASHINGTON HIGH SCHOOL**<br>2100 Parker Drive<br>West Washington, NV 89888<br>Academic Diploma, 1987 |
| | **UNIVERSITY OF THE MOUNTAINS**<br>Lake Hicauma, CA 12880<br>Bachelor of Science<br>Business Administration<br>1991 |
| **WORK EXPERIENCE:** | **SMITH & BAKER RETAILERS**<br>1 Black Oak Lane<br>West Washington, NV 89888<br><u>Assistant Buyer</u><br>Summer, 1988 - 1990 |
| | **UNIVERSITY OF THE MOUNTAINS**<br>Lake Hicauma, CA 12880<br><u>Student Activities Programming Assistant</u><br>Academic Year, 1989 - 1991 |
| | **FLOWERS ARE FOREVER**<br>Market Square<br>West Washington, NV 89888<br><u>Sales Clerk - Floral Arranger</u><br>Academic Year, 1987 - 1991 |
| **AWARDS AND SCHOOL ACTIVITIES:** | Varsity Basketball, Omega Phi Beta, Outstanding Student Volunteer, President's Honor Roll, Crisis Call Volunteer. |
| **SPECIAL SKILLS:** | Programming in BASIC and Pascal, Spanish (3 yrs.) |

**Figure 3-1.** Résumé

In comparison with memoranda created in prior chapters, this document is considerably harder to construct. In developing the first draft of the résumé you will:

1. Create and use new tabs settings and new margins settings;
2. Enter boldfaced characters while you type;
3. Center text on a line.

## FORMAT SETTINGS

People who work with word processors frequently find that many documents are similarly structured. In a university, a secretary may find that manuscripts in one discipline follow certain stylistic expectations (e.g., margins, line spacing, use of footnotes, etc.). A budget officer in a corporation may create project budgets with tables that use the same tab stops and margins. Students may find that term papers at their college are restricted to a particular style manual.

When there are recurring guidelines for the production of documents, it is often desirable to create a partial file with consistent line and page formatting commands that can be made a part of documents as soon as you begin to create them. You have seen that the Shift-F8 (Format) key can be used to modify tab settings, for example, once you have started a document. If tab settings change often within a document, modifying this ruler over and over takes unnecessary time, and your modifications may be inconsistent within documents and from one document to the next. You can create and save tab marker rulers and page format settings that are appropriate for the kinds of documents you work with. The resulting set of formatting values, called a WordPerfect Style (Alt-F8), can be retrieved at the start of each document that uses these settings.

### Load WordPerfect

Follow the instructions given in earlier chapters for loading WordPerfect and for making drive A the default drive.

### Defining the Style

First you must open a file that stores the codes used to facilitate the development of résumés. This set of codes is stored in a file called a style sheet. Press

**Alt-F8** Alternate and F8 key, to display the first Styles menu. WordPerfect may display a list of predesigned styles.

```
Styles

  Name          Type      Description

  Bibliogrphy   Paired    Bibliography
  Doc Init      Paired    Initialize Document Style
  Document      Outline   Document Style
  Pleading      Open      Header for numbered pleading paper
  Right Par     Outline   Right-Aligned Paragraph Numbers
  Tech Init     Open      Initialize Technical Style
  Technical     Outline   Technical Document Style

1 On; 2 Off; 3 Create; 4 Edit; 5 Delete; 6 Save; 7 Retrieve; 8 Update: 1
```

**Figure 3-2.** Styles Screen

3 To create a style. The Styles: Edit menu shown in Figure 3-3 appears.

```
Styles: Edit

     1 - Name

     2 - Type              Paired

     3 - Description

     4 - Codes

     5 - Enter             HRt

Selection: 0
```

**Figure 3-3.** Edit Styles Screen

To define the characteristics of your formatting, press

| | |
|---|---|
| **1** | To enter a name for the style |
| **RESUME** | The filename |
| **◄┘** | Enter key, to accept the filename |
| **2** | To declare a type. Paired, the default, refers to formatting of the sort that is always delimited, like boldface in which there is an opening and a closing code. Open refers to formatting codes like tabs and margins that do not require an ending code. The initial résumé settings would be open. |
| **2** | To define it as an open type |
| **3** | To enter a description of the style. You may use a maximum of fifty-four characters to describe the style. Type in *HARTLEY Resume 6/1/91* as the description. |
| **◄┘** | Enter key, to terminate the description |
| **4** | To prepare to place the desired formatting codes |

At this point you view a split screen nearly identical to the Reveal Codes window, with the cursor positioned in the upper left-hand corner, ready for you to begin placing formatting codes. You accomplish this by entering the appropriate menus and setting the values desired.

**Line Formatting**

The Line Format key is used to control the appearance of characters on a single line. Line formatting codes will be entered first. Press

| | |
|---|---|
| **Shift-F8** | The Format key, to see the Format menu (see Figure 2-3), which displays options for setting Line, Page, Document, and Other types of formatting codes |
| **1** | To see the Line Format menu |

```
Format: Line

     1 - Hyphenation                        No

     2 - Hyphenation Zone - Left            10%
                            Right           4%

     3 - Justification                      Full

     4 - Line Height                        Auto

     5 - Line Numbering                     No

     6 - Line Spacing                       1

     7 - Margins - Left                     1"
                   Right                    1"

     8 - Tab Set                            Rel: -1", every 0.5"

     9 - Widow/Orphan Protection            No


Selection: 0
```

Figure 3-4. Line Format Screen

8 To receive the tab settings ruler. You are going to change the tab settings to suit the résumé to be constructed. Using the procedures described in the previous chapter, modify the ruler so that it looks like in Figure 3-5.

```
L.........L..............L....L....L....L....L....L....L....L....L....L....L...
|    ^    |    ^    |    ^    |    ^    |    ^    |    ^    |    ^    |    ^
0"        +1"       +2"       +3"       +4"       +5"       +6"       +7"
Delete EOL (clear tabs); Enter Number (set tab); Del (clear tab);
Type; Left; Center; Right; Decimal; .= Dot Leader; Press Exit when done.
```

Figure 3-5. Revised Tab Settings

F7 The Exit key, to save the tab settings. You are returned to the Line Format menu.
◂┘ Enter key, to exit the Line Format screen and to return to the Format menu
◂┘ Enter key, to return to the Style version of the Reveal Codes window, to continue entering formatting codes. Notice your tab settings that now appear in the window.

### Page Formatting

Whereas the Line Formatting menu gave you options for describing how a single line should be patterned, the Page Format menu options shown in Figure 3-6 allow you to describe how the page should appear.

| | |
|---|---|
| **Shift-F8** | To again see the Format menu |
| **2** | To see the Page Format menu shown in Figure 3-6 |

```
Format: Page

     1 - Center Page (top to bottom)     No

     2 - Force Odd/Even Page

     3 - Headers

     4 - Footers

     5 - Margins - Top                   1"
                   Bottom                1"

     6 - Page Numbering

     7 - Paper Size                      8.5" x 11"
               Type                      Standard

     8 - Suppress (this page only)




Selection: 0
```

**Figure 3-6.** Page Format Screen

The settings to be used for the résumé file include only the choices 1, 6, and 8, which are covered shortly. Option 2 forces the number on the current page to be an odd or even number. This permits you, for example, to leave a gap in the numbering of pages to leave room to insert illustrations.

The headers (3) or footers (4) options place the same line of text at the top or bottom, respectively, of each page.

Option 5 is used to set the top and bottom margins in increments of one-hundredths of an inch. By default WordPerfect uses 1-inch margins.

Option 6 allows you to start numbering pages with a number other than 1. This allows you to create a large document, such as a book, in a group of files that can be printed separately and still have the pages numbered correctly. You can also reset a page number within a document. For instance, you may need to skip a page number to allow for a photograph to be inserted in the document.

With option 7 you identify the kind of form you are using for coordination with the form-handling capabilities of your printer.

To make the page format adjustments needed for the résumé file, type

| | |
|---|---|
| **6** | To set the position of the page number. If a page number position is not set, page numbers will not be printed. Figure 3-7 shows the Format: Page Numbering menu. |

```
Format: Page Numbering

     1 - New Page Number       1

     2 - Page Number Style     ^B

     3 - Insert Page Number

     4 - Page Number Position No page numbering










Selection: 0
```

**Figure 3-7.** Page Numbering Menu

| | |
|---|---|
| 4 | To set the page number position |
| 6 | To place the page numbers at the bottom center of the page. You are returned to the Format: Page Numbering menu. |
| F1 | Function key F1, to return to the Format: Page menu. |
| 1 | To center the page from top to bottom. The *No* on the screen changes to *Yes.* Since this format file may be used for very short résumés, this option places the résumé on the page with equally sized top and bottom margins. If the résumé exceeds one page, this code is ignored. |
| Y | **Y**es, center the page |
| 8 | To enter the Suppress Format menu shown in Figure 3-8 |

```
Format: Suppress (this page only)

     1 - Suppress All Page Numbering, Headers and Footers

     2 - Suppress Headers and Footers

     3 - Print Page Number at Bottom Center  No

     4 - Suppress Page Numbering             No

     5 - Suppress Header A                   No

     6 - Suppress Header B                   No

     7 - Suppress Footer A                   No

     8 - Suppress Footer B                   No




Selection: 0
```

**Figure 3-8.** Format Suppress Screen

| | |
|---|---|
| 1 | To turn off the page numbering and headers and footers entirely. Since some résumés have only one page, it is unnecessary to include a page number. The No is changed to Yes for options 3-8. |
| ↵ | Enter key, to exit the Format: Suppress menu |
| ↵ | Enter key, to exit the Format: Page menu |
| ↵ | Enter key, to exit the Format menu and return to the Style Codes window. You now view the codes entered: **[Pg Numbering:Bottom Center]** which places the page number in position 6, the bottom center; **[Center Pg]** which centers the page if necessary; **[Suppress:PgNum,HA,HB,FA,FB]** which suppresses the page numbering and headers and footers, if any, on the first page. |

**Saving the Style**

First exit the split screen mode for code/text entry by pressing

| | |
|---|---|
| **F7** | To return to the Style: Edit menu |
| **F7** | To return to the primary Style menu, where you now see the résumé style listed by name. The highlighting cursor is positioned on the Résumé Style. |
| **6** | To save the new Style as the beginning of a Style library |
| **STYLE.LIB** | The filename of the Style library |
| ↵ | Enter key |
| **1** | To turn on, or activate the style |

| | |
|---|---|
| Alt-F3 | To see that the codes entered have been discarded. You are now at the same point you would be if you had just booted WordPerfect, except that the file STYLE.LIB is now present on your files diskette. From the code **[Open Style:RESUME]** and from the tab settings, you see that the style has been retrieved. |
| Alt-F3 | To remove the Reveal Codes window |

**Retrieving the Style**

Assume that you had, in fact, just entered WordPerfect and that you wished to create a résumé. You would use this file (but don't since you already activated the style in the preceding steps) by typing

| | |
|---|---|
| Alt-F8 | The Style key, displaying the primary Style menu. Move the cursor to the style you want, or |
| 7 | To retrieve another Style library desired |
| STYLE.LIB | The filename of the Style library |
| ◄┘ | Enter key, to display the Style library desired. Position the cursor on RESUME. |
| 1 | To turn on, or activate, the style highlighted by the cursor |
| Alt-F3 | To see that the style has been retrieved. Notice the presence of the code **[Open Style:Resume]** and that the codes are in effect (notice the tab settings). |
| Alt-F3 | To remove the Reveal Codes window |

The Style feature becomes more powerful as additional styles are stored and grouped in libraries. It then provides substantial screen listings from which a variety of formats and text may be quickly selected for efficient document processing.

## LINE AND BLOCK MANIPULATIONS

### Centering and Changing the Font Attributes of a Line of Text

WordPerfect keeps track of the document's current margins and the font in effect. It can automatically compute the center point for the current margins and font, and insert text that is requested to be placed in the center. With the cursor at the beginning of the document, create and center the student's name by typing

| | |
|---|---|
| Ctrl-F8 | The Font key, to display the Font menu shown in Figure 3-9. |

```
1 Size; 2 Appearance; 3 Normal; 4 Base Font; 5 Print Color: 0
```

**Figure 3-9**. The Font Menu

| | |
|---|---|
| 1 | To display the Size Attribute menu shown in Figure 3-10. |

```
1 Suprscpt; 2 Subscpt; 3 Fine; 4 Small; 5 Large; 6 Vry Large; 7 Ext Large: 0
```

**Figure 3-10**. The Size Attribute Menu

Superscripts and subscripts are included on this menu because these characters are made smaller than regular type. These choices are placed here for that characteristic rather than for the spatial relationship to the type on the Normal line.

| | |
|---|---|
| 5 | To select Large font and return to the document |
| Ctrl-F8 | The Font key, to again display the Font menu |
| 2 | To display the Appearance Attribute menu shown in Figure 3-11 |

```
1 Bold 2 Undln 3 Dbl Und 4 Italc 5 Outln 6 Shadw 7 Sm Cap 8 Redln 9 Stkout: 0
```

**Figure 3-11.** Font Appearance Attributes

| | |
|---|---|
| 1 | To select Bold and to return to the document |
| Shift-F6 | Center key, to move the cursor to the center of the line |
| Caps Lock | Turns entry to uppercase |
| HARRIET HARTLEY | The student's name |
| Ctrl-F8 | The Font key, to display the Font menu |
| 3 | To return the font attributes to Normal (Shortcut: pressing the Right arrow key once at the end of the name also returns attributes to Normal) |
| ↵ | Enter key twice, to move to the next line of text to be entered |
| Caps Lock | Turns entry to lowercase |

You have learned about several features having to do with the Font key: Ctrl-F8.

1. The primary menu enables you to change the size of the base font.
2. You can change the appearance of the base font.
3. You can return the attributes to Normal.
4. You can change the base font by selecting from the fonts available.
5. You can change to printing colors within a text.

Bolding and underlining, the most commonly used attributes, may be selected in two ways: either through the Font key or by means of the F6 and F8 keys. The effect of these attribute choices depends, of course, upon the capabilities of your printer. You may learn many of your particular printer's capabilities, including its handling of all font attributes, by printing the PRINTER.TST file located on the Conversion WordPerfect diskette.

### Marking and Centering a Block of Text

The next three lines of the résumé are not in all uppercase, although individual words do begin with capital letters. You could enter and center these lines individually by pressing Shift-F6 and typing each line separately. This is perfectly acceptable. Another option, however, is to center a block of text.

There are several operations that WordPerfect allows on blocks of text, for instance, on these three lines, on two words, or on five characters. Among these operations are moving the block from one place in the file to another, deleting a block from the file, and copying the block to another location.

For illustrative purposes, type the three lines for the address at the left margin and hit the Enter key at the end of each line. Move the cursor to the left margin of the first of these lines (under the first *2* in *22*). Then, type

| | |
|---|---|
| Alt-F4 | The Block marking key |
| ↓ | Down arrow twice |

| | |
|---|---|
| **End** | End key, to fully mark the three lines |
| **Shift-F6** | The Centering key |
| **Y** | Yes, to center all three lines |

### Making In-Line Font Changes

When you created documents in the preceding chapters, several lines and phrases were underlined after the text had been entered in the document. In the résumé, the first line, as well as many other lines of text, are bolded. There is no point in typing in text to be bolded, for example, only to have to return to each line later to insert the bolding codes. Boldfacing and all other font/attribute changes can be managed as you are typing, as they were when you typed Harriet Hartley's name, or they can be added to a block of text marked with the Alt-F4 key, as was done with the centering of Harriet Hartley's address.

As you enter lines that are to be bolded, you will generally find it easiest to press the F6 key first, type the text to be bolded next, and press the F6 key again to turn bolding off. If you forget to bold some text, use the blocking procedure to bold it.

If you wish to underline existing text, block the text and use the F8 key instead.

### Entering Text

Enter the remainder of the sample résumé after you read the following information.

1. To embolden text, press the F6 key to begin the bolding, type the text, and press F6 to close the bolding. Text that is bolded can cover many lines.
2. Press Caps Lock on for appropriate lines.
3. Use the Tab key to place the cursor in the correct column for the *Education, Work Experience, Awards,* and *Special Skills* entry labels.
4. At the end of each entry line in *Education* and *Work Experience,* press the Enter key twice. The entries for *Professional Goal*, for *Awards and School Activities*, and for *Special Skills* should be broken with an Enter key since word wrap continues text at the left margin.
5. The underlining of text is accomplished in a fashion similar to bolding. Press F8 for underlining before you start typing the words to be underlined. Type the text. Then press F8 when you have typed the last letter to be underlined.

Enter the remainder of the résumé as shown in Figure 3-1. When it looks like the figure, go on to the next section.

## SUGGESTIONS FOR MODIFICATION

Harriet Hartley took her résumé to a career planning center for a counselor to critique it. The counselor suggested several changes to the résumé to convey the most important facts about Harriet's background to potential employers more effectively. Among the counselor's suggested changes are:

1. The career goal is too vague. It should be specific to a particular vocation.
2. The work experience section emphasizes the agencies Harriet had worked for, not the positions that she had held.
3. The work experiences for the university and the retail store should be reversed since they are not in descending chronological order.

**Deleting Blocks of Text**

Harriet decided to change the Professional Goal to *A marketing position in a computer company.* To make this change, place your cursor under the *T* in *To* in the sentence explaining Harriet's professional goal. Delete the two-line entry with a block delete. Press

| | |
|---|---|
| **Alt-F4** | The Block key, to begin the marking procedure |
| **↓** | Down arrow key twice |
| **End** | End key, to highlight the block defining the old sentence describing her career goal |
| **Del** | Delete key, to delete the block |
| **Y** | Yes, to confirm deletion |

The block is deleted from the file, but the block is also stored in the computer's memory. Recall the block of text from the Hold Area by pressing

| | |
|---|---|
| **F1** | Function key F1, Cancel/Undo, to highlight the last deleted text and undelete prompt |
| **F1** | Function key F1 a second time to cancel the retrieval |

The retrieval of deleted text can be made more than once. If you pressed the F1 key again, here or elsewhere, additional copies of the remembered text would be entered into the file. As more text is deleted, any of the previous three deletions can be retrieved. Do not do this. Continue by entering

**A marketing position in a computer**

| | |
|---|---|
| | The replacement text |
| **◄┘** | Enter key |
| **company** | The second line of text |
| **◄┘** | Enter key, to separate this section from the next section |

**Moving Blocks of Text**

The Alt-F4 combination used earlier to mark and center a block of text is also used to mark and move a block of text from one location to another. The employment date for Smith & Baker Retailers is chronologically earlier than the entry for the university. To place it correctly, it is not necessary to delete and retype the entry for Smith & Baker. Move it instead.

To move the text, place the cursor immediately under the *S* in *SMITH* and press

| | |
|---|---|
| **Alt-F4** | The Block key to start marking |
| **↓** | Down arrow six times, to highlight the block of text, the blank line, and the empty space up to the cursor on the line containing *UNIVERSITY OF THE MOUNTAINS* |
| **Ctrl-F4** | To receive the prompt shown in Figure 3-12. |

```
Move: 1 Block; 2 Tabular Column; 3 Rectangle: 0
```

**Figure 3-12.** The Move Menu

| | |
|---|---|
| 1 | The selection to move the block and receive the prompt shown in Figure 3-13. |

```
1 Move; 2 Copy; 3 Delete; 4 Append: 0
```

**Figure 3-13.**

| | |
|---|---|
| 1 | To cut the block out of its present position and retrieve it elsewhere. You receive the prompt,<br><br>Move cursor; press **Enter** to retrieve. |
| ↓ | Down arrow five times, to move the cursor under the first *F* in *FLOWERS ARE FOREVER* |
| ◂┘ | Enter key, to retrieve the block of text. The block is inserted between the university and florist shop entries. |

It takes practice to get the block move procedure to work efficiently. After any move you may have to follow up with editing keys to place the text where you want it.

The counselor suggested moving the position titles to the top of each work experience entry to emphasize what Harriet had done, not whom she had worked for. The movement of titles also uses the Alt-F4 keys. Place your cursor under the *S* in *Student Activities Programming Assistant,* and press

| | |
|---|---|
| **Alt-F4** | To begin marking the block |
| ↓ | Down arrow |
| **Ctrl-F4** | The Move key |
| **1** | To choose to move the block |
| **1** | To cut the text from the document |
| ↑ | Up arrow, to move the cursor under *U* in *UNIVERSITY* |
| ◂┘ | Enter key, to reinsert the block of text. The position title on your display is likely shown in a different color or intensity because WordPerfect is treating it as being bolded and underlined. |
| **Alt-F3** | The Reveal Codes key, to see the codes embedded in the text. Notice that the line begins with a **[Bold]** that is not closed until **[bold]** appears after *MOUNTAINS.* The code **[UND]** is highlighted by the cursor. |
| **Home,←** | Home and Left arrow, to highlight *W* |
| ← | Left arrow to highlight **[BOLD]** |
| **Del** | Delete key, to delete the opening and closing bolding codes. The position title now appears underlined, but the section title and the name of the university are no longer bolded. Block and make bold the job title using the instructions given earlier in the chapter. Do not rebold the name of the university. |
| **Alt-F3** | To remove the Reveal Codes window |

Because of the complexity of moving tabs and hard returns, text often does not line up neatly. When this occurs you have to edit with the Delete key and insert additional tabs.

Repeat the shifting of the position titles for the other jobs as well.

### Removing Bolding and Underlining Codes

The bolding and underlining should be changed to incorporate the suggestion of the counselor to emphasize positions and not the employers. Only the job titles should be bolded. Nothing should be underlined. In order to eliminate the codes that turn these fonts on and off, you must be able to see them. Type **Alt-F3** to open the Reveal Codes window and to see the embedded codes.

Use the arrow and other cursor movement keys to move the cursor to the location of the codes for bolding, **[BOLD]** and **[bold]**, and for underlining, **[UND]** and **[und]**. Delete the codes surrounding the employing organization and the position title with the Delete key or the Backspace key. To use the Delete key, the cursor must be positioned on the code to be deleted. To use the Backspace key, the cursor should be to the right of the code being removed. Deleting one of the codes in a pair also deletes the matching code. Type Alt-F3 to close the Reveal Codes window.

**Block Bolding and Changing Case**

It was recommended that the position held should be bolded and that it should be uppercased. To illustrate, place the cursor under the *S* in *Student Activities Programming Assistant,* and type

| | |
|---|---|
| **Alt-F4** | To begin marking the block |
| **End** | End key, to mark the line |
| **Shift-F3** | The (case) Switch key which gives you the opportunity to change all of the blocked letters to upper or lowercase |
| **1** | To convert the line to uppercase. The cursor moves to the end of the line and the blocking disappears. |
| **Alt-F4** | To begin marking the block |
| **Ctrl- ←** | Control and Left arrow three times to place the cursor under the *S* in *Student,* thereby highlighting the position title a second time |
| **F6** | The Bold key, which emboldens the line and cancels the blocking command |

Make these changes with the other position titles.

*SMITH & BAKER RETAILERS* should also be converted, but it should be altered so that each word has an initial capital letter and the rest of each word is lowercase. This is accomplished, for example, by placing the cursor under the *M* in *SMITH* and typing

| | |
|---|---|
| **Alt-F4** | To begin marking the block |
| **End** | End key, to mark the line |
| **←** | Left arrow, to remove block from address |
| **Shift-F3** | The (case) Switch key |
| **2** | To convert the line to lowercase and cancel blocking |

There is no way to quickly capitalize all of the first letters. It is possible to block each letter and convert it to uppercase, but this takes more keystrokes than simply deleting and replacing the letters. You can either delete each such letter and insert a capital or you can toggle the Insert key to typeover and replace the appropriate characters.

Effect this change with the other employers. The résumé should now look as it does in Figure 3-14.

**HARRIET HARTLEY**

22 Elm Street
West Washington, NV 89888
707-555-5665

**PROFESSIONAL GOAL:** A marketing position with a computer company.

**EDUCATION:**

**WEST WASHINGTON HIGH SCHOOL**
2100 Parker Drive
West Washington, NV 89888
Academic Diploma, 1987

**UNIVERSITY OF THE MOUNTAINS**
Lake Hicauma, CA 12880
Bachelor of Science
Business Administration
1991

**WORK EXPERIENCE:**

**STUDENT ACTIVITIES PROGRAMMING ASSISTANT**
University of the Mountains
Lake Hicauma, CA 12880
Academic Year, 1989 - 1991

**ASSISTANT BUYER**
Smith & Baker Retailers
1 Black Oak Lane
West Washington, NV 89888
Summer, 1988 - 1990

**SALES CLERK - FLORAL ARRANGER**
Flowers Are Forever
Market Square
West Washington, NV 89888
Academic Year, 1987 - 1991

**AWARDS AND SCHOOL ACTIVITIES:** Varsity Basketball, Omega Phi Beta, Outstanding Student Volunteer, President's Honor Roll, Crisis Call Volunteer.

**SPECIAL SKILLS:** Programming in BASIC and Pascal, Spanish (3 yrs.)

**Figure 3-14.** Completed Résumé.

## SAVING AND BACKING UP YOUR FILE

When your document has been completed, save your file by typing

| | |
|---|---|
| **F10** | The Save File key, for saving a document |
| **HARTLEY.RES** | The filename |
| ◄┘ | Enter key, to save your file |

Save your file again to your backup diskette by removing the diskette from drive A and replacing it with your backup diskette. The keystrokes this time are slightly different, since you have already specified the filename to the system.

| | |
|---|---|
| **F10** | The Save File key |
| ◄┘ | Enter key, to accept HARTLEY.RES as your filename and to save your file |

## PRINTING YOUR FILE

Now that the editing of the memorandum is finished and it has been saved, print out the document. In the next chapter you will revise and add text to the memorandum. To print out the file, type

| | |
|---|---|
| **Shift-F7** | To bring up the primary Print menu |
| **1** | To print the document |

## EXITING WORDPERFECT

Exit WordPerfect and return to DOS by pressing

| | |
|---|---|
| **F7** | The Exit key |
| **N** | To avoid saving your file again. If you wish you can combine saving a file and exiting WordPerfect by saving after pressing the F7 key. |
| **Y** | Yes, to exit WordPerfect. You can also respond *N* and when the screen is cleared, you can begin typing another document or you can exit as suggested. |

You will receive the DOS prompt at this point. You can turn the computer off if you wish.

## EXERCISES

A. Modify Harriet Hartley's résumé so that the two entries for education are reversed.

B. Create the following résumé using STYLE.LIB style named RESUME.

**DIXON MARS**

557 Waterbrook Farm Rd.
Covington Cove, NH 12111
323-718-9812

| | |
|---|---|
| **PROFESSIONAL GOAL:** | To employ my educational skills in the context of an exciting, upper-level, management position within an international corporation. |
| **EMPLOYMENT:** | **WEEKLY GAZETTE**<br>Newspaper Delivery Boy<br>High Falls, MA 37456<br>**BURGER HEAVEN**<br>Short Order Cook<br>High Falls, MA 37456 |
| **EDUCATION:** | **JOHNSON COUNTY JUNIOR COLLEGE**<br>A.S. in Business Administration<br>1987<br><br>**WILSON STATE UNIVERSITY**<br>B.A. in Public Administration<br>1989 |
| **AWARDS AND SCHOOL ACTIVITIES:** | Varsity Track (3 yrs.), Spanish Club (President), Alumni Solicitation Drive Volunteer, Ecology Club, Student Council (2 yrs.), Data Processing Management Association |
| **LANGUAGES SPOKEN:** | Spanish, Russian, German |

Modify the résumé to make it stronger by making the following changes:
--Change the professional goal to, *To work in the overseas division of an international hotel chain.*
--Delete the entire, weak employment history and replace it with a functional description of Mr. Mars' skills as follows:

| | |
|---|---|
| **FUNCTIONAL SKILLS:** | |
| **PLANNING:** | Developed an organized approach to the distribution of student government funds to approved organizations, reviewed all student organizational plans and projects, served as parliamentarian |
| **DIRECTING:** | Started the Ecology Club, created the aluminum can recycling effort, managed a trip to Mexico City during Spring break, served as a student coordinator for statewide telephone marathons |

**TRAVEL:** Lived in Madrid, Spain for 6 months, toured Japan for 2 weeks with family, attended the Study Abroad Program in Bonn, West Germany, organized trip to Mexico City, biked the Appalachian Trail

--Reverse the entries under education.
--Insert the section *INTERNATIONAL STUDIES COURSES:* and list the following courses:

ECON. 242 International Economics
MGRS. 342 International Business
PADM. 313 Independent Study: Trade Barriers in the Japanese Trade Market
LANG. 433 Russian Literature in Translation
PADM. 412 Comparative Study of Bureaucracies
Russian-4 language courses
German-6 language courses
Spanish-4 language courses

C. Use the Style RESUME to create your own résumé for use in job seeking.

# Chapter 4

# Using the Outline Feature

**Chapter Outline**



Writers in all fields find themselves outlining the text of documents they must prepare. Authors outline the chapters that compose the books they write; professionals in many fields prepare reports and proposals that are highly stylized in form and find that outlining the points to be made in each section is helpful; and students are often required to submit outlines of term papers before the papers themselves are submitted. This chapter is designed to show you how to effectively use the outlining capabilities of WordPerfect. This chapter is preparatory to the following chapter in which you type a short academic paper that is based on this chapter's outline. In this chapter you will:

1. Use the Date/Outline key to create an outline for a term paper;
2. Add and delete subsections of the outline;
3. Use the **[Par Num:Auto]** code to automatically number and letter different levels of an outline;
4. Move sections of an outline to new locations in the outline to see how WordPerfect automatically renumbers sections and subsections of an outline;
5. Use the Delete-to-end-of-line key;
6. Reset the tab settings to change the appearance of the outline;
7. Reset the outline's numbering style to meet your requirements.

The outline you will work with has been developed as the basis for a term paper by a student in a class on computers in business. The outline is incomplete since the student is still gathering research information to use in the paper. The outline currently looks like Figure 4-1.

```
THE PROS AND CONS OF WORD PROCESSING

I.    INTRODUCTION TO WORD PROCESSING

II.   DISADVANTAGES OF WORD PROCESSING
      A.    Cost
      B.    Professional Time Lost
      C.    Word Processing Inadequacies
      D.    Investments in Manual Typewriters

III.  ADVANTAGES OF WORD PROCESSING
      A.    Reduced Costs
      B.    Reduced Production Time
      C.    Higher Quality Output

IV.   CONCLUSION









Outline                                        Doc 1 Pg 1 Ln 3.33" Pos 1"
```

**Figure 4-1.** The Outline

DATE/OUTLINE KEY

Begin to create the outline by entering the title. Enter

Caps Lock — To set the keys to uppercase

THE PROS AND CONS OF WORD PROCESSING — The outline title, which is not numbered. Do not press the Enter key. If you did, press the Backspace key to return the cursor to the column immediately after the word *PROCESSING.*

One function of the Date/Outline key is the ability to turn the outlining feature off and on. Examine the Date/Outline menu by pressing

Shift-F5 — The Date/Outline key, to see the menu

```
1 Date Text; 2 Date Code; 3 Date Format; 4 Outline; 5 Para Num; 6 Define: 0
```

**Figure 4-2.** Date/Outline Menu

The only option to be used here is the fourth choice: Outline

4 — Presents the Outline menu

```
Outline: 1 On; 2 Off; 3 Move Family; 4 Copy Family; 5 Delete Family: 0
```

**Figure 4-3.** Outline Menu

| | |
|---|---|
| **1** | Set Outline on |

There is no obvious change on the screen except for the word Outline at the bottom left corner. Were you to look at the work area of the screen with the Reveal Codes key, Alt-F3, you would not see any different control codes either. From now on, however, every time you press the Enter key, WordPerfect automatically inserts a code that looks like **[Par Num:Auto]**. WordPerfect keeps track of these codes in such a way that it automatically letters or numbers each code according to the sequence in which it appears and according to the number of tabs that precede it. The number of tabs preceding the paragraph marking code determines the level of the item being numbered (Roman numeral, capital letter, Arabic numeral, etc.), whereas striking the function key F4 enables text entry at the particular level.

Begin to create the outline by pressing

| | |
|---|---|
| ◂┘ | Enter key once, to see the Roman numeral **I.** appear. The numeral appears on the line immediately underneath the title. A blank line should separate the title from the outline. |
| ◂┘ | Enter key, to insert a hard return in front of the command code |
| **F4** | The Indent key, to anchor the paragraph marker |
| **Alt-F3** | The Reveal Codes key, to see the codes **[Par Num:Auto][->Indent]** which denote the paragraph marker and the indented line key. The paragraph marker produces the **I.** and the indent key anchors the marker so it does not continue to move down the page with each pressing of the Enter key. |
| **Alt-F3** | Alternate key and function key F3, to remove the Reveal Codes window |

**INTRODUCTION TO WORD PROCESSING**

| | |
|---|---|
| | The first main section heading |
| ◂┘ | Enter key, to terminate the line and to insert a second paragraph marker that displays **II.** |
| ◂┘ | Enter key, to insert a blank line between major sections |
| **F4** | The Indent key, to anchor the second heading |

**DISADVANTAGES OF WORD PROCESSING**

| | |
|---|---|
| | The second heading |
| ◂┘ | Enter key, to terminate the line and to insert a third paragraph marker that displays **III.** The next entry, however, is to be a subsection of section **II.** |
| **Tab** | Tab key. The paragraph marker moves to the next level in and begins the subsection identification with an **A.** |
| **F4** | The Indent key, to anchor the marker |
| **Caps Lock** | To toggle caps off |
| **Cost** | The first subsection |
| ◂┘ | Enter key, to display **B.** with the cursor at the second level heading |
| **F4** | The Indent key |

**Professional Time Lost**

| | |
|---|---|
| | The next subsection |
| ◂┘ | Enter key, to display **C.** |

| | |
|---|---|
| **Tab** | Tab key, to intentionally put an extra and unnecessary tab into the text. The marker now shows **1.** |
| **Alt-F3** | The Reveal Codes key, to see the codes **[Tab][Tab][Par Num:Auto]**. You can see the extra tab and paragraph markers. Were you to try to delete the paragraph marker you would find it awkward to reinsert it without leaving an extra blank line. |
| **Shift-Tab** | Shift and Tab keys, to remove one tab marker. The paragraph marker displays **C.** Shift-Tab reduces the level for headings that have not been anchored with F4. |
| **Alt-F3** | Alternate key and function key F3, to remove the Reveal Codes window |
| **F4** | The Indent key |

**Word Processing Inadequacies**

The next subsection heading

### Arrow Keys Versus the Enter Key

When outlining has been turned on, you can move freely with the arrow keys without inserting new paragraph markers. If you press the Enter key, however, a paragraph marker is inserted. If you make a mistake, you can backspace or delete extra paragraph markers easily. This is described below.

Continue entering and editing the outline until it appears as it is displayed in Figure 4-1.

## EDITING THE OUTLINE

### Deleting Paragraph Markers

Codes produce the Roman and Arabic numerals as well as the letters that identify each section and subsection. If you need to delete a marker, you should use the Reveal Codes key to place the cursor on the paragraph marker. It is highlighted. Then delete the code with the Delete key. You may also delete the marker with the Backspace key if the marker is to the left of the cursor. You need only to delete the marker once even though the marker produces a multi-character display such as **III.** You may need to delete other codes and text on a line to modify the outline.

### Moving Sections of the Outline

After reviewing the outline, the student decides that the paper will probably end up with a positive conclusion about the future of word processing. The placement of the disadvantages of word processing at the beginning of the paper is undesirable from this point of view. The advantages should be listed first. Text in an outline can be physically moved around and WordPerfect automatically redetermines the correct section and subsection numbers. Reverse the order of the two sections by placing the cursor on the blank line between sections **II.** and **III.** and entering

| | |
|---|---|
| **Alt-F4** | The Block key |
| **↓** | Down arrow five times, to highlight four lines with text and the cursor appears on the blank line between sections **III.** and **IV.** |
| **Ctrl-F4** | The Move key, to see the prompt line shown in Figure 4-4. |

```
Move: 1 Block; 2 Tabular Column; 3 Rectangle: 0
```

Figure 4-4.

| | |
|---|---|
| 1 | Move the highlighted block. The prompt shown in Figure 4-5 appears. |

```
1 Move; 2 Copy; 3 Delete; 4 Append: 0
```

**Figure 4-5.**

| | |
|---|---|
| 1 | Move the block. The block of text is temporarily removed from the screen. The prompt line changes again to<br><br>Move cursor; press **Enter** to retrieve. |
| ↑ | Up arrow six times, to place the cursor on the blank line between sections **I.** and **II.** |
| ◄┘ | Enter key, to reinsert the previously cut text. Notice that all of the numbering markers for the sections and the subsections are correct. |

The movement and copying capabilities of the Control-F4 keys can be used in any document, not just in outlines.

**Adding Entries**

As the student continues reading about word processing, several additional subsections are found to be needed. A subsection is to be inserted after subsection II.C. The arrow keys enable you to move around without inserting new paragraph markers even though outline is toggled on. Move the cursor after the word *Output* and press

| | |
|---|---|
| ◄┘ | Enter key, to insert a hard return and to insert another subheading marker which displays **D.** |
| **F4** | The Indent key |
| **Improved Morale** | The new subsection |

Another subsection is missing which should occur after subsection **III.A.** Place your cursor after *Cost* and enter

| | |
|---|---|
| ◄┘ | Enter key, to insert a new subheading marker. Notice how the letters resequence automatically. |
| **F4** | The Indent key, to anchor the marker |
| **Vendor Dependence** | The heading to be inserted |

**Deletion to End of Line**

The student completing the outline has not been able to locate any references to support his assertion that the use of word processing improves morale. Since he cannot document this belief he will eliminate this topic from his paper. You have already deleted text one character and one word at a time. To delete an entire line one letter, or even one word, at a time is time-consuming. When the line contains embedded codes and the user is not careful in responding to prompts, default protections may allow some of the codes to remain on the line where they can cause difficulties later. WordPerfect allows you to delete all of the characters and codes on a line. Put the cursor on the line with the heading *Improved Morale* and type

| | |
|---|---|
| **Home, ←** | Home followed by Left arrow, to place the cursor at the beginning of the line |
| **Ctrl-End** | Delete-to-End-of-Line key, to remove all characters except the hard return code which keeps the blank line |
| **Del** | Delete key, to remove the hard return code |

The Delete-to-end-of-Line key can be used in all documents, not just in outlines. It deletes all characters and codes from the location of the cursor on the line. If it is in the middle of the line, text to the right of the cursor is deleted while the text to the left is left intact.

The entry in section III., **E. Investments in Manual Typewriters,** is another subsection that must be deleted because of a lack of documentation. Delete it in the same manner described above.

### Changing the Tab Settings

By utilizing the default tab settings, the section and subsection headings are farther apart than the student would like them to be. Since a topic outline has to be turned in before writing the paper, the student would like to use different tab settings. Press

| | |
|---|---|
| **Home,Home, ↑** | Home key twice followed by Up arrow, to move the cursor to the top line |
| **Shift-F8** | The Format key |
| **L** | Line formatting |
| **T** | Tab set, to change the Tab settings |

Review the tabs and rulers section of Chapter 2: Some Next Steps in Word Processing, to review how tab settings are altered. Change the tab ruler so that L tab settings are located at every fourth marker location up to +1.5 inches. The outline changes its spacing as you enter the L's. When you have inserted and deleted the L's required, press

| | |
|---|---|
| **F7** | The Exit key, to insert the tab settings in the document. Immediately, the spaces between the titles and paragraph marker displays are reduced, as are the indented distances for each level. |
| **↵** | Enter key, to exit the Format: Line screen |
| **↵** | Enter key, to exit the Format screen |

Your outline should now appear as it does in Figure 4-6. Print the outline.

```
THE PROS AND CONS OF WORD PROCESSING

I.    INTRODUCTION TO WORD PROCESSING

II.   ADVANTAGES OF WORD PROCESSING
      A.    Reduced Costs
      B.    Reduced Production Time
      C.    Higher Quality Output

III.  DISADVANTAGES OF WORD PROCESSING
      A.    Cost
      B.    Vendor Dependence
      C.    Professional Time Lost
      D.    Word Processing Inadequacies

IV.   CONCLUSION
```

**Figure 4-6.**

**Changing the Numbering Style**

Thus far, you have used the default numbering pattern for outlines. This pattern follows the order:

I. Roman numeral for sections;
    A. Capital letter for subsections;
        1. Arabic numeral for sub-subsections;
            a. Lowercase letter for sub-sub-subsections;
                (1) Enclosed Arabic for sub-sub-subsections;
                    (a) Enclosed lowercase letters . .;
                        i) Lowercase Roman numerals with right parenthesis ...;
                            a) Lowercase letters with right parenthesis ...

If you wish, you can alter the pattern by placing the cursor on the blank line above section I. and typing

| | |
|---|---|
| **Shift-F5** | The Date/Outline key |
| **6** | Define other options, to see Figure 4-7 |

```
Paragraph Number Definition

     1 - Starting Paragraph Number                    1
           (in legal style)
                                                       Levels
                                      1      2      3      4      5      6      7      8
     2 - Paragraph                    1.     a.     i.    (1)    (a)    (i)     1)     a)
     3 - Outline                      I.     A.     1.     a.    (1)    (a)     i)     a)
     4 - Legal (1.1.1)                1     .1     .1     .1     .1     .1     .1     .1
     5 - Bullets                      •      o      -      ■      *      +      •      x
     6 - User-defined

     Current Definition               I.     A.     1.     a.    (1)    (a)     i)     a)
     Attach Previous Level                   No     No     No     No     No     No     No

     7 - Enter Inserts Paragraph Number               Yes

     8 - Automatically Adjust to Current Level        Yes

     9 - Outline Style Name



Selection: 0
```

**Figure 4-7.** Paragraph Definition Screen

At this point you have four choices open to you. Choice 2, Paragraph, exhibits the Arabic numerals first, the lowercase alphabetic characters second, and so on. Choice 3 is the outline numbering that you have been using. Choice 5 switches the level marking symbols to those displayed on the screen. Choice 6, User-defined, allows you to design the display style you would like to use. You will convert the outline to the legal style, choice 4, by entering

| | |
|---|---|
| 4 | To select legal numbering |
| ↵ | Enter key, to exit the Paragraph Number Definition screen |
| ↵ | Enter key, to exit the Date/Outline screen |
| + | Grey plus key, to move to the bottom of the page. This immediately converts the displays to the legal style even though the paragraph marker codes embedded in the text have not been altered. |

The outline appears as shown in Figure 4-8.

```
THE PROS AND CONS OF WORD PROCESSING

1    INTRODUCTION TO WORD PROCESSING

2    ADVANTAGES OF WORD PROCESSING
     2.1 Reduced Costs
     2.2 Reduced Production Time
     2.3 Higher Quality Output

3    DISADVANTAGES OF WORD PROCESSING
     3.1 Cost
     3.2 Vendor Dependence
     3.3 Professional Time Lost
     3.4 Word Processing Inadequacies

4    CONCLUSION








Outline                                        Doc 1 Pg 1 Ln 1" Pos 1"
```

**Figure 4-8.** Legal Style Outline

### SAVING AND BACKING UP THE FILE

Save your file by typing

| | |
|---|---|
| **F10** | The Save key |
| **OUTLINE** | The filename |
| ◄┘ | Enter key, to accept *OUTLINE* as the filename |

Save your file again to your backup diskette by removing the diskette from drive A and replacing it with your backup diskette. Save the file to the backup diskette with the same keystrokes, except that the filename is supplied by the system this time.

### PRINTING THE FILE

Now that the editing of the outline is finished and it has been saved, print the document. To print the file, type

| | |
|---|---|
| **Shift-F7** | To obtain the prompt |
| **1** | To print the document |

## EXITING WORDPERFECT

Exit WordPerfect by pressing

| | |
|---|---|
| F7 | The Exit key |
| N | To avoid saving your file again |
| Y | Yes, to exit WordPerfect or type *N* and begin typing another document |

## EXERCISES

A. Outline this chapter of this book by hand. Then create the outline using the outline feature. Convert the outline to a legal style of numbering.

B. Create the following outline for a student term paper on computer data storage:

```
COMPUTER MEMORIES

I.   Random Access Memory
       A.   Also called RAM, Main, Core storage
       B.   Very fast
       C.   Volatile
              1.   Lost when power is turned off
              2.   Recoverable only in certain computers
II.  Cache Memory
       A.   High-speed storage
       B.   Found close to RAM
       C.   Stores data that are expected to be used shortly
       D.   Avoids long search times
III. Secondary Storage
       A.   Disk drives
       B.   Cassettes and tapes
       C.   Older technologies
              1.   Cards
              2.   Drums
              3.   Paper tapes
```

C. Create the following outline. After you have entered the outline, use the Other Options choice of the Outline key to set the level designator numbers and letters as they are displayed. Reset the tab markers so that an *L* appears at columns 10, 12, 14, 16, and 18 so the outline is spaced as shown.

FLOPPY DISK DRIVES

A. General Points
    I. Somewhat flexible
    II. Ruined by heat, contaminants, and magnetism
    III. Removable
B. Density
    I. Normal (out-of-date) for single-sided disks
    II. Double Density
        i. Introduced with double-sided disks
        ii. Stores 360 Kb of data
    III. Quad Density
        i. Found on 80286 microcomputers
        ii. Stores 1.2 Mb of data
        iii. Cannot be read by double density drives
        iv. Can read double density disks

# Chapter 5

# Advanced WordPerfect Usage

**Chapter Outline**



The documents created thus far have demonstrated many WordPerfect features. You are now able to produce many types of documents. Still, there are many other features that you can use to give your documents a professional look. While not all of the features can be dealt with here, you will be able to experiment with the remaining features on your own if you wish to do so. In this chapter you will:

1. Use hanging paragraphs in which a number can appear inside of the temporarily widened left margin;
2. Center individual lines and blocks of lines;
3. Use automatic hyphenation;
4. Insert hard page breaks;
5. Insert commands that alter the appearance of a page. The commands can be used for footnoting, for changing margins, for using header and footer lines, and for changing line spacing.

The document in this chapter is a short paper. On the surface it appears easy. It uses some features that you have used before, such as font changes and line centering. The indented paragraphs (lettered subsections) are different and, after the initial text has been entered, you will be adding features such as footnotes, headers, and page numbers. These features are available in any sophisticated word processing software.

Figure 5-1 is a short paper produced by a student in an introductory computing class. Initially, this paper will be created with WordPerfect's default tab ruler.

**THE PROS AND CONS OF WORD PROCESSING**
<Your Name>

I. INTRODUCTION TO WORD PROCESSING

There are many ways in which computers can operate on textual information. Text editors are normally used to create programs or data to be processed by programs. Text editors are not adapted to preparing letters, term papers and other documents. They have little capability for formatting the text in a variety of styles. Some programming languages, most notably Snobol, are adept at analyzing text files, but they are almost useless for preparing normal business and personal communications.

Word processors and text formatters, software designed to produce written documents, are improving steadily. Word processors are generally categorized as displaying a document on the computer monitor in much the same appearance as that of the printed document. Text formatters, on the other hand, produce files in which there are large numbers of "dot" commands that will be used by the formatter to guide printing. The file looks substantially different from the eventual printed document since word filling, footnotes, margin settings and type faces are not arranged by the formatter until the document is printed.

II. ADVANTAGES OF WORD PROCESSING

Word processing software capabilities have been developing rapidly. The number of word processing packages is large and the number of persons who use word processors in their work and for personal usage is also substantial. Many people do not begin to utilize all of the capabilities their word processors possess, but they are likely to realize at least some of the advantages noted by some of the writers who have studied the use of word processing in industry. Among the advantages of word processors and text formatters are the following:

A. Reduced Cost. Errors can be corrected rapidly, greatly reducing the time involved in producing a document. Of greater importance, revisions to documents are significantly less costly than are complete retypings of documents.

B. Reduced Production Time. When documents are revised, the editor need only proofread the altered text for accuracy. Previously acceptable text will not have changed. This is different from typed text in which an entire document must be reread to be certain that new errors have not slipped in.

C. Efficient Staff Usage. Documents can be entered by relatively untrained, lower-cost typists. Corrections and complex formatting can be turned over to more skilled word processing operators in later revisions.

D. Higher Quality Output. Because revisions are easy to make, managers and other writers are less hesitant to revise and reprint documents until they are precisely correct.

III. DISADVANTAGES OF WORD PROCESSING

Even though there is almost universal agreement that word processing is an essential element in the modern business environment, there are drawbacks to its usage. These disadvantages include:

A. Cost. Word processors are significantly more expensive to buy and maintain than are standard typewriters. Personnel must be trained to use the word processors.

B. Vendor Dependence. Each word processing software package is unique. Document files cannot be easily shared, if at all, between different word processors or word processing software packages. Once a company has committed itself to one approach, change is costly.

C. Professional Time Lost. Many people who used to dictate or write out documents by hand find that they prefer to type their own drafts of documents. They may then find that they prefer to do the editing themselves because it is faster than writing notes about changes to be made and then having to explain the notes to a secretary. To be certain the document is correct, they print it out. Before you know it a professional being paid $40,000 a year is doing the job of a $15,000 a year secretary.

D. Word Processing Inadequacies. There are many differences among word processors. Even with the best word processors there will be special capabilities like equation formatting, table production and interfaces with type setting equipment that are not available. The production of some documents may be difficult and the organization may find that several different word processors will be needed to meet all of the

**Figure 5-1.**

## TEXT MANIPULATIONS

### Centering and Boldfacing

The first line is bolded and centered. Do this by pressing

| | |
|---|---|
| **Shift-F6** | The Center key combination |
| **F6** | The Bold key, to turn bolding on. Notice the change in color or intensity of the Pos number. |
| **Caps Lock** | To turn letters to uppercase. Then type |

**THE PROS AND CONS OF WORD PROCESSING**

| | |
|---|---|
| | The paper's title |
| **F6** | To turn bolding off |
| ◂┘ | Enter key, to complete the centering of the line |

Enter and center your name (without bolding) in the same manner. Press the Enter key twice to move the cursor down two lines.

**Underlining**

The text on the line beginning with the Roman numeral *I.* is to be underlined. To enter this line place your cursor at the left margin and type

| | |
|---|---|
| **I.** | The section designator |
| **Space,Space** | Space bar twice, to insert two spaces between the section number and the heading |
| **F8** | The Underline key, to turn underlining on. Notice the change in appearance of the Pos number. Then type |

**INTRODUCTION TO WORD PROCESSING**

| | |
|---|---|
| | The subsection heading |
| **F8** | To turn underlining off |
| **◄┘** | Enter key |

Use the same technique for underlining the two additional lines with Roman numerals as they occur in the text. Enter the first three paragraphs and stop when you reach the end of the paragraph immediately before the first subsection, A.

## SAVING YOUR FILE

Before proceeding further, save your file by entering

| | |
|---|---|
| **F10** | The Save key |
| **paper** | The filename |
| **◄┘** | Enter |

As you work through the following instructions for modifying the paper, save the file whenever you reach a point of completion. Then, if you make a mistake, you can remove the degraded version of the file that you see on your screen by exiting with the F7 key and not saving the file. Respond *N* to the prompt asking whether you wish to exit WordPerfect, and after a blank work screen appears, retrieve the preserved version of PAPER with the Shift-F10 key combination.

## HANGING PARAGRAPHS

The paragraphs marked A, B, C, etc., are called hanging paragraphs. This is because the label is hanging in the left margin that has been temporarily widened. The typing of the hanging paragraphs will be difficult if you use the Tab key for indentation. Using the Tab key after each word wrap, you would have to move the cursor to the left margin to enter additional tabs to place the text at the correct location. In addition, if you start editing the text by inserting and deleting words, you will find that the tab markers will have to be adjusted constantly.

To employ a hanging paragraph, the F4 key is used to create a temporary indentation that will remain in effect until the Enter key is pressed. Skip a line between paragraphs and create the first such paragraph by typing

| | |
|---|---|
| **A.** | The subsection label |
| **F4** | The Indent key |
| **F8** | The Underline key, to turn underlining on |
| **Reduced Costs** | The subsection heading to be underlined |
| **F8** | The Underline key, to turn underlining off |
| **.** | A period that is not underlined |
| **Space, Space** | Space bar twice |

**Errors can be corrected rapidly . . . .**

| | |
|---|---|
| | The text for the hanging paragraph |
| ◄┘ | Enter, pressed once at the end of the paragraph. The cursor returns to the default left margin. |

Enter the remaining hanging paragraphs in the same fashion. When the paper is complete, save it with the Save Files key, F10.

## PRINTING THE FILE

When the paper is complete, print it by pressing

| | |
|---|---|
| **Shift-F7** | The Print Document key |
| **1** | To print the full text |

## LINE FORMATTING COMMANDS

WordPerfect is almost entirely a "What-you-see-is-what-you-get" word processor. So far, the documents you have created have printed out as they appeared on the screen. The current document is lacking in some features that you have probably begun to sense are needed. There are additional controls you can use over the final appearance.

You have already used some page formatting controls when you added page numbers, suppressed the printing of page numbers on the first page, and centered résumés on a page. Now you will use some added features.

### Margin Changes

WordPerfect uses default margins of 1 inch from the left edge of the paper and 1 inch from the right edge of the paper. You may wish to alter the margin for several reasons. If you use paper that is not 8 1/2 by 11 inches there is more or less space on a line than can be filled. If you change the character size to compressed type, or if you use proportional type, you can get more characters on a line and the left margin is closer to the left edge of the paper. Margins are easily changed. To change the margin for this paper, move the cursor to the top of the document and enter

| | |
|---|---|
| **Shift-F8** | The Format key, to display the Formatting Prompt screen |
| **1** | Line formatting (or press *L*) |
| **7** | Margins change (or press *M*) |
| **1.5** | To increase the left margin, thereby decreasing the size of the printed line |
| ◄┘ | Enter key |
| **1.5** | To increase the right margin, again decreasing the size of the printed line |
| **F7** | The Exit key, to return to the document. |

| | |
|---|---|
| + | Grey plus sign, to reformat the visible and the nonvisible portions of the document. |

**Line Spacing**

It is desirable to print all of your drafts of a large document in single space to conserve paper and printing time. Once you have finalized the paper size, however, you may wish to shift to double spacing. Do this by returning your cursor to the top of the document, then enter

| | |
|---|---|
| **Shift-F8** | The Format key |
| **1** | Line, to alter the line formatting |
| **6** | Line spacing |
| **2** | To set double spacing on from the top |
| **◄┘** | Enter key |
| **F7** | Exit key. The change in line spacing is immediately visible. |

Notice that extra lines, between paragraphs for instance, cause WordPerfect to show three blank lines. These lines are not needed in a double spaced document. **Locate the extra lines throughout the document and delete them.**

**Hyphenation**

By default WordPerfect does not automatically hyphenate any words. When hyphenation is turned off, the default condition, complete words are wrapped to the next line if they do not fit on the previous line. This does not always produce a satisfactory document. If hyphenation is off, a line with very few words will have larger than desirable spaces between the words. In some cases, depending upon your printer's capabilities, these spaces can be fine-tuned by resetting kerning and right-justification values from the Format menus. A kern is an extension to the body of a letter and kerning is the ability of WordPerfect to overlap the kerns of letters into the spaces of other letters. In all cases, however, when hyphenation is on, words will be hyphenated and fewer large spaces will appear between words.

Turning hyphenation on enables WordPerfect to suggest where words should be broken. Hyphens inserted in a word are soft hyphens because WordPerfect will change them if a paragraph is reformatted or if the margins of a document change and the complete word is able to be printed on a single line. There are two limits that define the full hyphenation zone. The zone looks like that pictured in Figure 5-2.

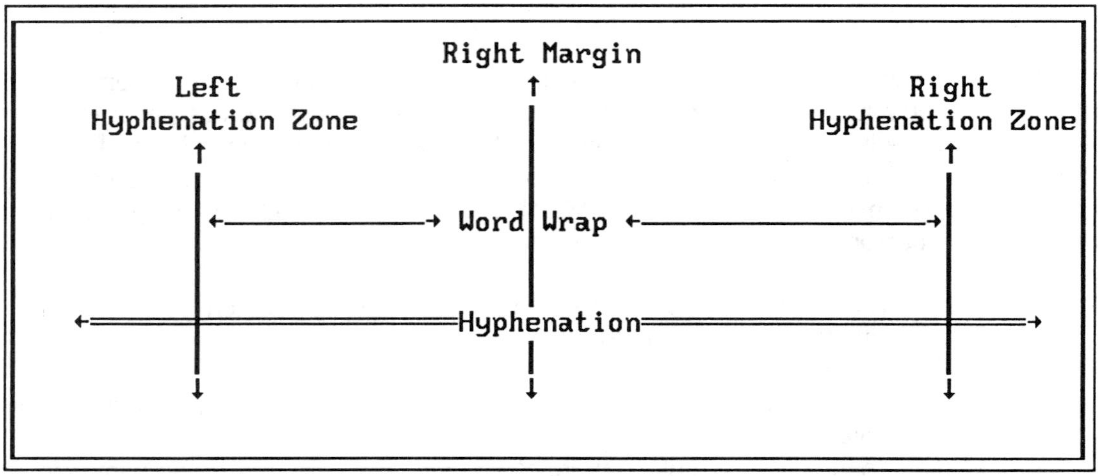


**Figure 5-2.** Hyphenation Zones

When hyphenation is turned on, WordPerfect follows these rules.

1. A word that ends before the right margin will not be hyphenated.
2. A word that begins after the right margin is word wrapped.
3. A word that begins after the left hyphenation zone and extends beyond the right margin will be wrapped to the next line.
4. A word that begins at or before the left hyphenation zone and extends beyond the right margin will be hyphenated.
5. Hyphenation will be suggested in syllables, falling between the left and right hyphenation zones.

By reducing the size of the hyphenation zone, more words will be forced by WordPerfect to be hyphenated.

Make sure that your cursor is at the top of the document and enter

| | |
|---|---|
| **Shift-F8** | The Format key |
| **1** | Line Format. Hyphenation is shown to be off. The hyphenation zone, also called the H-Zone, is shown to be 10% and 4%. |
| **1** | Hyphenation. |
| **Y** | Yes, turn hyphenation on |
| **2** | Hyphenation Zone, to change the default H-Zone of 10% and 4% |
| **6** | The new left hyphenation zone that will be a smaller percentage of the print line's width |
| ◄┘ | Enter key |
| ◄┘ | Enter key. The right hyphenation zone will not be changed |
| ◄┘ | Enter key, to exit the Line Format screen |
| **F7** | Exit key, to exit the Format screen |
| + | Grey plus sign as necessary, to move through the document. Although WordPerfect may select a different word for different documents and WordPerfect setups, you will be prompted to position the hyphen for some words. The prompt may appear as<br><br>**Position hyphen; Press ESC stead_ily**<br><br>The prompt is allowing you to choose whether the flashing underscore is where you would like to place the hyphen. Your options at this point are to press:<br>1. the Left Arrow key to move to a more appropriate breaking point;<br>2. ESC to insert the hyphen;<br>3. F1, the Cancel key, to prevent hyphenation.<br>If you use the arrow key to move the cursor to a new hyphenation location, you press Escape when you have found that location. If you press Cancel, a Slash (/) will be placed in front of the word when you look at it on the Reveal Codes window (Alt-F3), but the Slash will not be seen in the normal work area, nor will the Slash print out. The Slash simply indicates that the word has been explicitly prevented from being hyphenated. Press |
| **Esc** | To hyphenate the word as suggested by WordPerfect. The document returns to the screen and the word is shown hyphenated. |
| **Grey +** | Grey plus key several times. WordPerfect will identify other words that need to be hyphenated. As you are prompted to do so, select locations in which to hyphenate these words. |

Continue pressing the grey plus key and as you progress through the document hyphenate the remaining words. Because the hyphenation zone has been set somewhat arbitrarily, some words will be forced to break that you might prefer to have left un-hyphenated. This is acceptable since this is only an exercise.

## PAGE FORMATTING COMMANDS

### Headers and Footers

It is often desirable on long documents to have common identification lines at the top and/or bottom of each page. Identification lines at the top of the page are called headers, and those at the bottom are called footers. You might want to identify the pages with one or more identifiers such as the date, the words "Draft" or "Top Secret," or the title of the document. You have already used the Format key (Shift-F8) that allows the entry of a footer, and you have seen the Format Screen that appears after pressing the Format key. Place the cursor at the top of the document and press

| | |
|---|---|
| **Shift-F8** | To call up the Format screen |
| 2 | Page formatting |
| 4 | Footers, or press *F,* to enter the first part of a footer line |
| 1 | To enter the left footer (Footer A) |
| 2 | To have the footer appear on every page |
| **Word Processing J. Knowsit** | |
| | The footer to be printed. Use appropriate function and cursor movement keys to center, bold, underline or otherwise format the footer. To print the page number as part of the footer or header, press Ctrl-B at the correct location. |
| F7 | Exit key; exit footer entry. The Page Format screen returns the message "FA Every Page." A position A footer will be printed on every page of the document. |
| 8 | To suppress the printing of the footer on the first page since the title and name are already on the page |
| 3 | To print only the page number at the bottom center of first page. The footer is not printed. |
| Y | Yes, accept this option |
| ◄┘ | Enter, to exit the Suppress screen |

### Page Numbers

Most documents should include page numbers to facilitate the reader's task of locating important sections, to make notes about points raised and so forth. Page numbers are requested from the Page Format screen.

| | |
|---|---|
| 6 | Page numbering (or press 7) |
| 4 | To set the page number position |
| 3 | To select the upper right corner of the page. Other options are available. Page numbering will begin at the position of the page location code, consequently it is important that this code is inserted at the top of the document and before any text that is to be printed. |
| F7 | Exit key, to return to the document |

**Footnotes**

In typing, the placement of footnotes is always a challenge. You must keep track of the number of lines you have typed and leave enough space to put the footnote(s) at the bottom of the page. If you are using footers, correct placement of the footnote is a big chore. Small miscalculations may force you to retype an entire page. WordPerfect takes care of these calculations for you.

Assume that you wished to include a footnote citation to document a conclusion in the first paragraph in Figure 5-1. Do this by placing your cursor immediately behind the period following the word *communications* at the end of the first paragraph. Press

**Ctrl-F7** — The Footnote key

**1** — Footnote, to begin to create a footnote that appears at the bottom of the current page, the first page in this case. Note: do not confuse a footnote with an endnote. The footnote appears at the bottom of the current page while the endnote appears at the end of the document.

**1** — Create, to start a new footnote. Do not erase the *1* that appears next. This is the footnote number created by WordPerfect.

**F4** — Function key F4 to indent the footnote's text

**Wells, M. T. "Approaches to Word Processing," <u>Journal of Spurious Results</u>, Vol. 10, Number 13, May 1989, pp. 2224.**

The text for the footnote. Some of the text in the footnote is underlined with the F8 key, and you may be prompted for a hyphen for the word *Processing.*

**F7** — The Exit key, to close the footnote. A footnote number, 1, appears at the location of the cursor. This number will be superscripted automatically if your printer is capable of superscripting.

**Alt-F3** — The Reveal Codes key

**←** — Left arrow, to see the code

**[Footnote:1;[Note Num][->Indent] Wells, M. T. "Approaches ... ]**

that creates a footnote and note number that produces the number 1. The beginning of the footnote can also be seen in the window but nowhere in the document until it is printed.

**Alt-F3** — Alternate key and function key F3 pressed simultaneously, to close the Reveal Codes window. Additional footnotes could be added in the same fashion throughout the document.

**HARD PAGE BREAKS**

As you look at your document you may see that at the top of page 2, one line containing part of a sentence appears. A document looks better if at least two lines of the text follow immediately after the heading introducing that section and if at least two lines of a paragraph carry over to the following page. It is desirable to force the printer to move to the next page before the previous line is printed. The command for forcing the printer to eject to the next page is called a hard page break. A soft page break, seen on your screen as a row of dotted lines, is the page break which is entered by WordPerfect when it determines that it has printed the maximum number of lines on a page as specified by the page formatting commands. Put a hard page break in your document by placing your cursor after the third line from the bottom of page 2 and pressing

**Ctrl-◂┘** The Hard Page Break key. A row of equal signs appears that represents a hard page break.
**Alt-F3** The Reveal Codes key, to see the code **[HPg]** noting that the writer caused the page to break at this point
**Del** Delete key, to delete the now unneeded blank line created with **[HRt]**
**Alt-F3** The Alternate and F3 keys pressed simultaneously, to remove the Reveal Codes window

A hard page break will not be affected by the reformatting of the document. If a hard break is inserted and reformatting caused the break to appear two lines from the top of a page, a break would still occur. Sometimes this is acceptable since you may wish to ensure that the next item, a table perhaps, begins at the top of the page regardless of the amount of white space left on the previous page.

## SAVING AND BACKING UP THE FILE

Save your file by typing

**F10** The key for saving a document
**PAPER2** Your filename
**◂┘** Enter, to enter PAPER2 as the filename

Save your file again to your backup diskette by removing the diskette from drive A and replacing it with your backup diskette. Save the file to the backup diskette with the same keystrokes, except that this time the system prompts you with the filename.

## THE PRINT CONTROL SCREEN

In all of the preceding chapters, the printing of a document was completed by selecting the first choice on the following menu that was displayed when you pressed the Shift and F7 keys. The selection of **1** printed the entire document as it currently appeared on the screen. In this section you will learn how to print one document while working on another document.

**F10** The Save key
**ERASEME** A new filename, cleverly selected so you avoid replacing PAPER2; the filename will suggest erasing the file at a later date
**◂┘** Enter

Call up the Print Control screen by pressing

**Shift-F7** The Print key, to see the menu shown in Figure 5-3.

```
Print

     1 - Full Document
     2 - Page
     3 - Document on Disk
     4 - Control Printer
     5 - Multiple Pages
     6 - View Document
     7 - Initialize Printer


Options

     S - Select Printer                   Epson LQ-500
     B - Binding Offset                   0"
     N - Number of Copies                 1
     U - Multiple Copies Generated by     WordPerfect
     G - Graphics Quality                 Medium
     T - Text Quality                     High




Selection: 0
```

**Figure 5-3.** Print Control Screen

The Print Control screen offers such a wide variety of ways in which to alter the basic print command that all of the options cannot be described in this book. In summary, the Print Control section has choices numbered 1 through 7, S, B, N, U, G, and T. Some of the primary choices are described in Figure 5-4.

| CHOICE | FUNCTION |
|---|---|
| P | Prints the page the cursor is currently on. |
| D | Prints the document that is on your diskette, not the one which is currently on your screen and in RAM. After pressing *D* you would be prompted for the filename, including the drive and directory if these are different from the current defaults. |
| C | Controls the printer to cancel one or all printing commands that have been queued up. |
| V | Views the document the way WordPerfect will print it. This will enable you to see the pages with page numbers, footers, etc. before you waste paper and the time in printing a document that is incorrect. |
| S | Selects from among the printers that have drivers installed on your copy of WordPerfect. |
| N | Alters the number of copies of the document that can be printed with one command. |

**Figure 5-4.** Selected Print Control Options

The Current Job and Job List sections of the screen provide you with information about the last print job submitted, as well as about the queue of print jobs that have been submitted in previous print commands. Continue to print the file ERASEME with

| | |
|---|---|
| D | Print a document on the disk command, which then prompts you with<br><br>**Document Name:_** |
| A:ERASEME | The file to be printed which is currently found on drive A. The drive letter need not be typed if the default drive is B. |
| ◄┘ | Enter key |
| ◄┘ | Enter key, to print all of the pages in the document. If you did not wish to print the entire document, you can print individual pages. If you entered *5*, you would print only page 5. If you entered *5-10*, you would print pages 5 through 10. If you entered *5-*, you would print the document from page 5 to the end. If you entered *5-10,15* you would print pages 5 through 10 and 15. |

When the default entry of 0 returns as the Selection on the Print Control, press

| | |
|---|---|
| ◄┘ | Enter, to return to the WordPerfect work screen |

## NONJUSTIFIED RIGHT MARGINS

The paper you have just printed has, by default, a justified right margin. Spaces are inserted between words and punctuation to evenly space them across the line. Look carefully at the words in the first paragraph and you may detect extra space that has been inserted throughout the lines in order to force the last printed character to the last column. Many people prefer, especially when narrow margins are in use, to use a ragged right margin in which no blanks are inserted and in which the line stops as soon as the last character is printed. See what this looks like by returning the cursor to the top of the document and pressing

| | |
|---|---|
| **Shift-F8** | The Format key |
| **1** | Line |
| **3** | Justification |
| **1** | Left, to justify the left margin, but not the right margin |
| **F7** | The Exit key, to exit the Line Format screen |

Print the document again to see the difference the removal of the justification option makes.

## VIEWING THE DOCUMENT

WordPerfect is not exactly a "What-you-see-is-what-you-get" word processor. You normally do not see page numbers, footers, or footnotes, for example, even though these will appear in the final document. You may wish to check these and other features before you print the document. Spotting an error before printing the document will save you the time and expense of unnecessary printing. To see what the document looks like without printing it, move the cursor to the beginning of the document and enter

| | |
|---|---|
| **Shift-F7** | The Print key |
| **6** | View, to see the full first page of the document |
| **PgDn** | The Page Down key, to see the next page. You may use the PgUp and PgDn keys to look at the entire document. When you have finished viewing the document as it will eventually appear, press |
| **F7** | The Exit key, to return to the WordPerfect editing screen |

## EXITING WORDPERFECT

Exit WordPerfect by typing

| | |
|---|---|
| **F7** | The Exit key |
| **Y** | **Y**es, save the file |
| **PAPER3** | The filename |
| **↵** | Enter. You may receive requests to adjust the hyphens in some of the words before the document is saved. Do so with the Escape and Left Arrow keys. |
| **Y** | **Y**es, to exit WordPerfect, or type *N* and begin the exercises |

## EXERCISES

A. Use WordPerfect to produce your next term paper or class assignment.

B. Choose sections of this or some other book that uses underlining, bolding, indented paragraphs, columns, or other special formatting features, and try to reproduce them with WordPerfect.

C. Using the paper, "The Pros and Cons of Word Processing," produced in this chapter, indent four entries under the paragraph entitled, *A. Reduced Costs*. Revise the paragraph to include the following subentries. Press the Tab key before the subsection number and the Indent key after the subsection number.

A. Reduced Costs. Errors can be corrected rapidly, greatly reducing the time involved in producing a document. Of greater importance, a revision of a document is significantly less costly than is a complete retyping of the document.
   1. Cheap printers can produce draft work quickly and inexpensively,
   2. Expensive laser printers can be used to produce final documents,
   3. Proofreaders do not have to reread entire documents,
   4. Document files can be accessed by some typesetting machines. Therefore, documents do not have to be keyed in again.

Then use the same ruler to add entries beneath the paragraph entitled, *C. Higher Quality Output,* so that it appears as:

C. Higher Quality Output. Because revisions are easy to make, managers and other writers are less hesitant to revise and reprint documents until they are precisely correct.
   1. Laser printers can be acquired to produce cleaner, neater output,
   2. Spelling checkers, style checkers, and thesauruses can be used to assure correct output,
   3. Documents can be merged and reused, thereby reducing the chance for the introduction of errors,
   4. Data from worksheets and databases can be added without retyping.

Find and delete the margin change, **[L/R Mar:1.5",6.5"]**, the line spacing code **[LnSpacing:2]**, and the hard page break, **[HPg]**. Save the revised document as PAPER4. Print the document.

# Chapter 6

# Advanced Editing Aids: The Spelling Checker and the Thesaurus

**Chapter Outline**



Word processing software programs like WordPerfect are unable, at this point in their development, to have a substantial impact on the qualitative aspects of writing. Other types of software might provide help in arranging paragraphs to be sure that they are in correct order. They cannot determine whether you have incorrectly selected *their* when *there* was the homonym of choice. Was the theme of your paper strongly presented? Did you exercise forceful usage of adjectives and adverbs? Were the best arguments brought to bear on your point? Is the punctuation placed in the right location? On these and many other important aspects of writing, WordPerfect is silent.

WordPerfect does not have these features, but it does have two other capabilities that you will appreciate having to enhance the quality of your writing: a spelling checker and a thesaurus. In this chapter you will:

1. Use the built-in thesaurus to suggest words that can replace words already in a document;
2. Use the thesaurus to suggest words that can replace a word that you are thinking about, but have not yet entered into the document;
3. Use the spelling checker to correct improperly typed words in a document.

## THE THESAURUS

Writing an effective document depends on many things, not the least of which is the use of appropriate words to achieve the intended effects on the reader. Words must be selected carefully. Though a word may seem to be adequate when first used in a sentence, you may later wish to replace it with a word that has a stronger, more precise meaning.

Without WordPerfect you would probably look up a word in a printed thesaurus to find a list of synonyms which have approximately the same meaning as the word you started with and antonyms which mean the opposite. The entry for the word *approximately* in the thesaurus, for example, proposes words like *about, almost,* and *roughly* as possible substitutes. If one of the suggested words sounds better in the context of your writing, you would replace *approximately* with that word.

WordPerfect allows you to do this manual search-and-replace sequence rapidly and conveniently. The procedure to use the thesaurus is so smooth that you use it often.

### Replacing an Existing Word

Load WordPerfect and retrieve the file *PAPER* that was written in the last chapter. Place the cursor under any letter in the word *ways* on the first line. Assume that you would like to see if you can find a word that is somewhat more distinctive. Type

Alt-F1 — The Thesaurus key. As shown in Figure 6-1, the lower three-fourths of the screen is replaced by a three-column window that displays synonyms of the word above the cursor.

```
     I.   INTRODUCTION TO WORD PROCESSING

          There are many ways in which computers can operate
     on textual information.  Text editors are normally used
     to create programs or data to be processed by programs.
way=(n)
  1 A ·custom
    B ·habit
    C ·manner
    D ·practice

  2 E ·means
    F ·method
    G ·procedure
    H ·process
    I ·technique

  3 J ·avenue
    K ·course
    L ·direction
    M ·route

1 Replace Word; 2 View Doc; 3 Look Up Word; 4 Clear Column: 0
```

**Figure 6-1**. Sample Thesaurus Screen

The word itself is repeated in a label, **way (n)**, where the (**n**) indicates that the words displayed are synonymous with the noun form. Other words may display (**n**), (**ant**) for antonym, or (**v**) for verb. The thesaurus menu that appears is shown in Figure 6-2.

```
1 Replace Word; 2 View Doc; 3 Look Up Word; 4 Clear Column: 0
```

**Figure 6-2**. Thesaurus Menu

Thirteen possible synonyms are suggested for *ways.* Each synonym is preceded by a letter. Substitute the word *method* for *ways* by typing

| | |
|---|---|
| **1** | To select the menu choice Replace Word |
| **◄┘** | Enter key, to select the word *method.* Either an upper or lowercase letter can be typed. The Thesaurus window disappears and the substitution is made in the document. |
| **s** | To make *method* plural |

Move the cursor to place it beneath the word *Reduced* in subsection B of section II. It is generally held that repetitions of a word in close proximity detract from the word's usefulness. Find a substitute by pressing

| | |
|---|---|
| **Alt-F1** | The Thesaurus key, to recall the Thesaurus screen. The synonyms for the verb form of reduced are under the **reduced(v)** label and the antonyms of reduced are under **reduced(ant)** |
| **1** | To replace the word *Reduced* |
| **a** | To select *decrease* as the substitute. Notice that the first letter of *Decrease* is capitalized just as was the first letter in *Reduced.* |
| **d** | To make the word past tense |

**Expanding the Search**

The word *complex* appears in subsection C of section II. Again, assume that you wish to find a synonym for this word. Place your cursor under *complex* and type

| | |
|---|---|
| **Alt-F1** | The Thesaurus key. Perhaps seeing the list does not suggest an adequate replacement. |
| **3** | To begin to look up a synonym of *intricate.* Words on the screen that are preceded by dots have synonyms that can be looked up. Words without dots in front of them cannot be searched for any further. |
| **C** | The letter preceding *intricate.* A complete word could be typed here and that word would be looked up. |
| **◄┘** | Enter key. A list of synonyms for *intricate* appears in the second column and each is preceded by a letter. The letters no longer appear in the first column. |
| **←** | Left arrow, to move the letters to the first column. This is to show that you can still choose a replacement from the original list. |
| **→** | Right arrow, to see the second list |
| **1** | To start the replace operation |
| **F** | To replace the word *complex* with *involved* |

**Viewing the Document**

Sometimes the Thesaurus window does not reveal enough of a word's context for you to determine which of several synonyms would be suitable. You may wish to see more of the document. Place your cursor under the word *skilled* in the same sentence and type

| | |
|---|---|
| **Alt-F1** | The Thesaurus key. The list of possible substitutions appears. |
| **2** | To open the view document option. Observe that the cursor appears on the line. |
| **↑** | Up arrow five times, to see additional lines above the line containing *typists* |
| **↓** | Down arrow as necessary to expose more lines below |

| | |
|---|---|
| **F7** | The Exit key, to return to the substitutions list where *skilled* is still highlighted |
| **1** | To start the replacement operation |
| **J** | To substitute *talent* for *skill* |
| **ed** | To change to past tense |
| **←** | Left arrow, to put the cursor under the *o* in *over* |
| **Ctrl-Backspace** | To delete *over* |

When you move the cursor vertically, the line is reformatted.

### Looking Up a Word

So far, each of the examples used began with a word that has already been typed into the document. If you have a need as you are typing to find an alternative for a word you feel is weak, you may wish to look it up immediately, rather than typing in the questionable word first. Place your cursor behind the period of the last sentence of the document and type

| | |
|---|---|
| **Space,Space** | Space bar twice, to separate the previous sentence from the next one to be typed |

**In addition to increased sales, it is likely that the word processing industry will introduce**

| | |
|---|---|
| | The beginning of a new sentence with a space following introduce |
| **Alt-F1** | The Thesaurus key |
| **significant** | The word to be looked up |
| **↵** | Enter key |
| **1** | To replace, even though *significant* has not been typed into the document |
| **A** | To enter *important* |

**improvements in desktop publishing that will sustain the momentum already present.**

| | |
|---|---|
| | To end the sentence |

## THE SPELLING CHECKER

Proofreading is a crucial skill. Even excellent spellers make typographical errors or come across words whose spelling they cannot recall. For poor spellers, proofreading is even more critical. But good proofreading assumes that you recognize an incorrectly spelled word when you see it. It also assumes that you look carefully at each and every word and not become distracted from time to time. Of course, few of us, when proofreading a very long paper, can meet both of these conditions. WordPerfect has the answer to this problem: a spelling checker that checks each and every word in your document to see if it recognizes it. If it does not, it offers you opportunities: to change it, if it is, indeed, spelled incorrectly; to ignore the unrecognized spelling; or, if the word is spelled correctly, to add the word to WordPerfect's list of words it recognizes so that the word is not flagged as incorrect in the future.

### Introducing Some Intentional Errors

For illustrative purposes, enter the following words and character strings in the text of the term paper. These errors will be corrected with the spelling checker afterwards. Enter

1. *tany* instead of many in paragraph 1;
2. *XYZ* after *which* in front of *Text,* and after *letters*, all in paragraph 1;

3. *Chemo-therapy* after *steadily.* at the end of sentence 1 of the second paragraph;
4. *Are* behind the word *are* and in front of the word *generally* in paragraph 2;
5. Change *capabilities* to *capaibilities* in paragraph 3, and *noted* to *nted,* which is also in paragraph 3.

Press

| | |
|---|---|
| **Home,Home, ↑** | To return the cursor to the top of the document |

**Spell Check by Word**

At times you may enter a word, look at it, and question whether it is properly spelled. If there is any doubt in your mind you can check the spelling for this one word immediately. You do not have to check the spelling of all words in your document. Before proceeding, place your cursor under the *t* in *operate* in the beginning sentence of the first paragraph. Then press

| | |
|---|---|
| **Del** | The Delete key, to delete the *t*. The word is obviously spelled incorrectly. Leave the cursor under the final *e*. |
| **Ctrl-F2** | The Spell key. You receive the prompt |

```
Check: 1 Word; 2 Page; 3 Document; 4 New Sup. Dictionary; 5 Look Up; 6 Count: 0
```

**Figure 6-3.** Spell Screen Menu

| | |
|---|---|
| 1 | To check the spelling of the word above the cursor. A Spell Screen is shown in Figure 6-4. A list of words preceded by letters appears on the screen and *operae* is put into reverse video to indicate that the word is incorrectly spelled. The words that are suggested as possible substitutes are similar in spelling to *operae.* That is, by adding, transposing, or changing one or two letters in the original word, the suggested word could be constructed. Since the word is misspelled, various alternatives that are given may be very different from the desired spelling. A new prompt appears with the choices that are shown in Figure 6-3. Not all of these choices will be demonstrated. |

```
                    <Your Name>

   I.   INTRODUCTION TO WORD PROCESSING

        There are mny methods in which XYZ computers can
   operae on textual information.  Editors are normally
   used to create programs or data to be processed by
   programs.  XYZ Text editors are not adapted to prepar-
   ing letters XYZ, term papers and other documents.  They
   have little capability for formatting the text in a
   variety of styles.  Some programming languages, most
                                          Doc 1 Pg 1 Ln 2" Pos 1.5"
▲  {  ▲  ▲  ▲  ▲  ▲  ▲  ▲  ▲  ▲  ▲  }  ▲  ▲  ▲

 A. opera             B. operas             C. operate
 D. opere             E. apiary             F. aporia
 G. aporiae           H. appear             I. upper
 J. yapper            K. yauper

Not Found: 1 Skip Once; 2 Skip; 3 Add; 4 Edit; 5 Look Up; 6 Ignore Numbers: 0
```

**Figure 6-4.** Sample Spell Screen

The options that are available through the spell screen are described in Figure 6-5.

| OPTION | MEANING |
|---|---|
| Skip Once | Do not change this word, but go on to the next misspelled word. If this word appears again, pause to see if it should be changed at that location. |
| Skip | Do not change this word. Store its spelling and if this word appears again, ignore it. |
| Add | Keep in a dictionary that is in addition to the built-in dictionary of about 100,000 words. The second dictionary can contain technical terms and proper names that you may use, but that many other people would not. |
| Edit | Change the word that is highlighted. |
| Look Up | Identify similarly spelled words using the "wild card" characters * and ? (as in DOS) to display the correct spelling; also identify words that sound like the currently highlighted word. |
| Ignore Numbers | Pass over values in the spelling check. |

**Figure 6-5.** Spell Screen Choices

| | |
|---|---|
| **C** | To replace the incorrectly spelled word with choice C in the suggested word list |
| **F1** | The Cancel key, to notify WordPerfect to discontinue the search for other misspelled words |

**Add Word**

You will now utilize several additional commands with the Spell menu. With the cursor at the top of the document, enter

| | |
|---|---|
| **Ctrl-F2** | The Spell key |
| **3** | To check spelling throughout the term paper. If you have introduced other spelling errors than those specifically included, you may have to read ahead to see how to fix an incorrect spelling. |

The spelling checker may stop at your name and place it in reverse video. Not surprisingly, this word is not contained in the 100,000-word dictionary provided by WordPerfect because your first and last names are proper nouns. The spelling dictionary has very few names. The student plans to continue to use WordPerfect for many years and decides that it would be a waste of time to have the spelling checker find his name each and every time it appears in one of his writings. WordPerfect keeps a second dictionary containing words that this user feels are sufficiently repetitive to store them. This second dictionary can house proper names and technical terms that many other people do not use frequently. To illustrate how to add a word, press

| | |
|---|---|
| **3** | The add-a-word choice. The word is added to the previously empty supplementary dictionary. |

When the words *Snobol, desktop*, and *Chemo-* appear, repeat this command.

**Edit Word**

The spelling checker moves on to the next word that it does not recognize, *tany.* This word is certainly spelled incorrectly. Choose

| | |
|---|---|
| **4** | To edit the word. The cursor appears under the *t* and the highlighting disappears. |
| **Del** | Delete key, to remove the *t* |
| **m** | The letter *m,* to correct the spelling |
| **F7** | The Exit key, to note that the word has been corrected. WordPerfect will not accept another incorrect spelling, but returns the prompt that includes the edit option to allow you to try to fix it again. |

As they appear, correct the spelling of *capaibilities* and *nted* with this option.

**Skip Word**

The next word highlighted by WordPerfect is *XYZ.* Assume that this is another technical term, the name of a company, that is spelled correctly. Since this word may not appear in future papers it is desirable to skip it rather than to add it to the dictionary. There are two ways to do this: to skip it once but flag future occurrences of XYZ, and to skip it throughout the remainder of the document. To skip it once, enter

| | |
|---|---|
| **1** | To skip XYZ once. The second occurrence is highlighted. |
| **2** | To skip all future occurrences of XYZ. The third occurrence is not flagged as unrecognizable by WordPerfect. |

**Double Word**

It is common to type double words both by accident and by design. It is not always clearly wrong to have double words. For instance, *That that was wrong is clear!* is a correctly written sentence, while the highlighted instance of *are are* is certainly an error. WordPerfect finds double words. If you feel the word pair is apt, skip the occurrence by typing either a *1* or a *2.* Delete one of the words, the second, by pressing

| | |
|---|---|
| **3** | To delete the undesired second word |

Choice 4 allows you to change one of the words by editing it. This choice would enable you to change *tip tip* to *tip top* without retyping two of the letters. You can prevent further double word checking with choice 5.

**Word Count**

At the end of its search, WordPerfect reports how many words are in the document, or on a page if the search is restricted to one page. If only a word count is desired, you can choose Count from the spelling checker's original prompt.

There is no reason to save this file. If you wish to save the file, however, follow the instructions contained in earlier chapters.

## PRINTING THE FILE

Now that the editing of the term paper is finished and it has been saved, print out the document by typing

| | |
|---|---|
| **Shift-F7** | To obtain the Print prompt |
| **1** | To print the document |

## EXITING WORDPERFECT

Exit WordPerfect by typing

| | |
|---|---|
| **F7** | The Exit key |
| **N** | **N**o, do not save the file |
| **Y** | **Y**es, to exit WordPerfect, or type *N* to begin the exercises |

## EXERCISES

A. Make a copy of the term paper produced in Chapter 5: Advanced WordPerfect Usage, and name it TEST1.
   1. Change the spelling of twenty words scattered throughout the paper to make them incorrect.
   2. Introduce three double words.

3. Use global search-and-replace to change the spelling of *the* to %*w*&.
4. Use the spelling checker to correct all of the changes made except for %*w*&, which should be skipped as the spelling checker works through the text.

B. Make a copy of the term paper produced in Chapter 5: Advanced WordPerfect Usage, and name it TEST2. Exchange the following words with one suggested by the thesaurus:

| | | |
|---|---|---|
| create | capability | adept |
| different | possess | accuracy |
| vendor | certain | expensive |

C. Use the spelling checker to examine and correct one of the documents you prepared in earlier chapters. Change ten words you used with words suggested by the thesaurus.

D. Create a paragraph with the intention of using the text that follows. Before you type the boldfaced words, however, use the thesaurus to look up the bolded word and use one of the alternatives proposed, if there is one. Sometimes a root word can be found when a word with modified endings can be located.

The **wildly angry** man **whirled** a chain **around** his head **menacingly**. As the **crowd** scattered, the sheriff **drew** his **revolver**. **"Stop,"** he said, **pointing** his **weapon** at the man. The man **meekly** put down the **chain** and **cried**.

# Chapter 7

# Merging Files: The Form Letter

**Chapter Outline**



The ability to merge files and create a personalized form letter is a primary advantage of word processing. The creation of merged files saves considerable time. In little more than the time it takes to create one letter, you can create hundreds, all identically correct and perfectly formatted. In addition, once the proper files have been set up, they can quickly be modified for later applications. Merged files can be used to create mass mailings and multiple letters of application for jobs, and to fill out forms.

This chapter will extend your knowledge of WordPerfect by showing you how to:

1. Create a primary file consisting of the form letter and merge codes which direct the merge;
2. Create a secondary file containing the records for the merge;
3. Use the Merge Codes menu to begin the merge;
4. Use keyboard entry in a merge;
5. Manage blank field names in a merge.

## THE FORM LETTER

You have, no doubt, received form letters. A form letter is personalized with your name and address, although the body of the letter is identical to that sent to many others. The form letter consists of variable, personalized text and unchanging text, which remains identical from one letter to the next. Each kind of information is stored in a separate file. The variable information, often consisting of names and addresses, is stored in the secondary file, also called a data file, containing the data that will be used to fill in the blanks of the form letter. Unchanging information, consisting of the body of the letter and other elements, is stored in the primary, or main, file. Merging combines these two files into a third file which consists of the product of the merge: all of the finished letters.

## THE PRIMARY FILE

Previously you created Harriet Hartley's résumé. Imagine that Ms. Hartley wishes to send her résumé to many firms to secure a position. With merging, she can save time and effort. Figure 7-1 shows the primary file that must be created. This file contains the text of her letter and the merge codes which control placement of the variable information. Merge field codes are entered through a Merge Codes menu found on function key Shift-F9. Although codes like **{FIELD}1~** appear on the screen, these codes cannot be typed on the work screen; they must be entered through the Merge Codes menu.

```
{DATE}

{FIELD}1~
{FIELD}2~
{FIELD}3~
{FIELD}4~

Dear {FIELD}6~:

I am writing in the hope that I might be considered for an entry
level marketing position with your company.

Having just graduated from the University of the Mountains with a
B. S. in Business Administration, I am eager to begin my
professional career.  Based upon my experience and qualifications,
summarized in the attached resume, I believe I could make a
valuable contribution to your firm.

I can be reached by telephone at 707-555-5665 during working hours.
I would welcome the chance to discuss employment possibilities with
you and would be happy to appear in person for an interview you
might schedule at your convenience.

I look forward to talking with you.

Sincerely,



Harriet Hartley
22 Elm Street
West Washington, NV 89888

Enclosure: Resume
```

**Figure 7-1.**

### Overview: Field Numbers and Text

Notice that the primary file begins with a number of merge codes: **{FIELD}1~**, **{FIELD}2~**, and so forth. The merge codes indicate to WordPerfect which field values are to be merged and where they are to be merged. In this case, field values 1, 2, and 3 are to merge at the beginning of the letter, and field value 6 is to appear in the salutation line, after the word *Dear.* After that point the primary file is all standard text.

### Creating the Primary File

With the cursor positioned at the top left corner of the opening WordPerfect screen, press

| | |
|---|---|
| **Shift-F9** | The Merge Codes key, to display the Merge Codes menu. You should now see this menu at the bottom of your screen, with the cursor blinking in the position after the colon. |

```
1 Field; 2 End Record; 3 Input; 4 Page Off; 5 Next Record; 6 More: 0
```

**Figure 7-2.** Merge Codes Menu

| | |
|---|---|
| **1** | To select the F or Field code. You are prompted for the field number to be inserted. |
| **1** | To select Field Number 1, the first field to be put into the secondary file which is yet to be created. The first field will contain the full name of the individual receiving the letter. |
| ◄┘ | Enter key, to execute the selection. **{FIELD}1~** appears on the screen |
| ◄┘ | Enter key, to move the cursor to the next line |
| **Shift-F9** | The Merge Codes key, to display the Merge Codes menu |
| **1** | To select the Field Code |
| **2** | To select Field Number 2. This field in the secondary file will contain the individual's title. |
| ◄┘ | Enter key, to execute the selection |
| ◄┘ | Enter key, to move the cursor to the next line |
| **Shift-F9** | The Merge Codes key, to display the Merge Codes menu |
| **F** | To select the Field Code |
| **3** | To select Field Number 3. This field in the secondary file will contain the name of the organization of the person being written to. |
| ◄┘ | Enter key, to execute the selection |
| ◄┘ | Enter key twice, to create a blank line |
| **Dear** | As the beginning of the salutation |
| **Space** | To separate words |
| **Shift-F9** | The Merge Codes key, to display the Merge Codes menu |
| **1** | To select the Field Code |
| **6** | To select Field Number 6 |
| ◄┘ | Enter key, to execute the selection. **{FIELD}6~** will appear on the screen. This field contains the name to be used in the salutation of the letter. |
| **:** | To put in the colon ending the salutation |
| ◄┘ | Enter key twice, to create a blank line before the beginning of the body of the letter |

Now type in the rest of the letter as standard text. Save the file as **LETTER.PF**. Exit the document but not WordPerfect, leaving the blank beginning WordPerfect screen.

## THE SECONDARY FILE

Shown below as Figure 7-3 is the secondary or data file.

```
Dr. Everett Murchison{END FIELD}
Director of Marketing{END FIELD}
Collegiate Computing Systems{END FIELD}
1028 Westport Boulevard
Islandview, California 98765{END FIELD}
707 441-6652{END FIELD}
Dr. Murchison{END FIELD}
{END RECORD}
=======================================================
Mr. G.N. Dayton{END FIELD}
Chief Executive Officer{END FIELD}
National Information Systems{END FIELD}
555 Industrial Parkway
Census, Ohio 29534{END FIELD}
299 600-0000{END FIELD}
Mr. Dayton{END FIELD}
{END RECORD}
=======================================================
Mr. Edson Baker{END FIELD}
President{END FIELD}
Smith & Baker Retailers{END FIELD}
1 Black Oak Lane
West Washington, Nevada 89888{END FIELD}
{END FIELD}
Edson{END FIELD}
{END RECORD}
=======================================================
```

**Figure 7-3.** Secondary File

### Overview: Records, Field Numbers, and Field Values

The secondary file consists of a number of records, each containing specific information of different kinds. In the example above, the records consist of the following fields: (1) name, (2) title, (3) company, (4) street address/city/state/ZIP code, (5) phone number, and (6) the name (two with courtesy titles). Notice that each field is terminated with the merge code **{END FIELD}** and that each record is terminated with **{END RECORD}** followed by a hard page break. Also notice that the address field is entered on several lines before the **{END FIELD}** is found. A field's value is considered to be everything between the previous field's **{END FIELD}** and the field's own **{END FIELD}**, regardless of the number of lines separating the two codes. If you omit an **{END FIELD}** code, the contents of two fields would be combined into one field.

Although the field numbers are not displayed, the fields are designated by number according to their order. That is, WordPerfect counts the fields in each record beginning with the number 1. Field value number 1, therefore, is whatever text precedes the first merge code **{END FIELD}** in the record. If you forget to include a field **{END FIELD}** code even when the field is empty of information, WordPerfect will assume that the data from the next field should be used. Consequently, if the data for a field were not available, say a person's title, an **{END FIELD}** should be entered on a line by itself to indicate that there was no value to be included in this location. The information that is entered for each field is called the field's value. Mr. Edson Baker is the value of field 1 for record number 3.

**Creating the Secondary File**

With the cursor positioned at the top left-most column of the opening WordPerfect screen, type

**Dr. Everett Murchison**

As the first field value of the first record

**F9** — The Merge R key, to insert the first **{END FIELD}** code, indicating the end of the first field value. Notice that the cursor automatically wraps, by inserting a hard return, to the next line. It is important that an extra hard return is not placed at the end of the field, since that would interfere with the proper functioning of the merge.

**Director of Marketing**

As the second field value of the first record

**F9** — The Merge R key, to terminate the field and to insert the second **{END FIELD}** code. Again, the cursor wraps to the next line.

**Collegiate Computing Systems**

As the third field value

**F9** — The Merge R key, to insert the third **{END FIELD}** code

**1028 Westport Boulevard**

As the first line of the fourth field value

**↵** — Enter key, to move the cursor to the next line. Notice in this case that we wish to create a two-line field value. We are combining the street address and city/state/ZIP as one field value, separated by a hard return. In this case we want the hard return to become a permanent part of the field value: whenever we wish to merge field value 3, we are assuming we will want it to appear on two separate lines with a hard return following the street address.

**Islandview, California 98765**

As the second line of the fourth field value

| | |
|---|---|
| **F9** | The Merge R key, to insert the fourth **{END FIELD}** code |
| **707 441-6652** | As the fifth field value. This field will not be used in this letter. |
| **F9** | The Merge R key, to insert the fifth **{END FIELD}** code |
| **Dr. Murchison** | As the sixth field value, the salutation |
| **F9** | The Merge R key, to insert the sixth **{END FIELD}** code. Now you must terminate the record with the **{END RECORD}** code. |
| **Shift-F9** | The Merge Codes key |
| **2** | Notice that when the code is inserted, a hard page break is also inserted and the cursor automatically wraps to the beginning of the next line. You are now ready to type in the second record. |

Type the second and third records in precisely the same way, with one exception. Notice that the phone number field value (number five) in the third record is blank. In cases where there is no value to enter, the Merge code (**{END FIELD}**) is still entered on the line by itself. This allows WordPerfect to keep track of correct field numbers throughout a record. All records must have the same number of fields, even if some are blank. If you accidentally omit a field, correct your omission by placing the cursor to the left of the **{END FIELD}** on the previous line. Then press F9. This will insert a new merge code symbol at the end of that line and will move the cursor to the next line. Add the field's missing value.

## EXITING THE DOCUMENT

Once you have entered all three records and have insured that they are identical to those shown in Figure 7-3, enter

| | |
|---|---|
| **F7** | The Exit key |
| **Y** | Yes, save the file |
| **RECORDS.SF** | The name of the file |
| ◄┘ | Enter key |
| **N** | No, do not exit WordPerfect, and leave the WordPerfect screen displayed |

## MERGING THE FILES

If the screen has not been cleared, repeat the instructions for exiting shown above. You should not begin the merge if text remains on the WordPerfect editing screen. You are now ready to merge the two files. Press

| | |
|---|---|
| **Ctrl-F9** | The Merge/Sort key, to display the Merge/Sort menu. You should see this display at the bottom of the screen: |

```
1 Merge; 2 Sort; 3 Convert Old Merge Codes: 0
```

**Figure 7-4.** Merge/Sort Menu

| | |
|---|---|
| **1** | To select Merge and to display the prompt for primary file |
| **LETTER.PF** | The name of the primary file |
| ◄┘ | To start the merge process and to receive the prompt for secondary file |
| **RECORDS.SF** | The name of the secondary file |
| ◄┘ | To execute the merge process |

WordPerfect now merges the information from the RECORDS.SF file with the text and codes in the LETTER.PF file, producing a third file on the screen (which has not been written to disk) consisting of three letters separated by hard page breaks.

If you managed the entire merge correctly, the address and salutation lines of the letters should look like Figure 7-5.

```
February 15, 1991

Dr. Everett Murchison
Director of Marketing
Collegiate Computing Systems
1028 Westport Boulevard
Islandview, California 98765

Dear Dr. Murchison:
     :
     :
     :
========================================
February 15, 1991

Mr. G.N. Dayton
Chief Executive Officer
National Information Systems
555 Industrial Parkway
Census, Ohio 29534

Dear Mr. Dayton:
     :
     :
     :
========================================
February 15, 1991

Mr. Edson Baker
President
Smith & Baker Retailers
1 Black Oak Lane
West Washington, Nevada 89888

Dear Edson:
     :
     :
     :
```

**Figure 7-5.**

Notice that in the third record, WordPerfect correctly counted past the blank, fifth field value to use Edson in the salutation. You have mastered one of the techniques for handling blank field values in the secondary file. You will learn the other one, how to apply this to the primary file, in the next section.

## PRINTING THE LETTERS

The merged letters are printed with the Shift and F7 keys in the same way any other document is printed. Print the letters.

Since you can always reproduce these letters by merging the primary and secondary files again, there is no reason to save the merged letters. Use the F7 key to exit from the document without saving it, but return to the opening WordPerfect screen.

## FURTHER HELPFUL MERGE OPERATIONS

In this section you will learn three more merge codes, which allow you to insert the current date automatically, to pause for keyboard entry, and to display a message. We will modify Harriet Hartley's cover letter so that it looks like Figure 7-6.

```
{DATE}

{FIELD}1~
{FIELD}2~
{FIELD}3~
{FIELD}4~

Dear {FIELD}6~:

In response to your recent advertisement in {INPUT}Cite ad source~, I am
writing in the hope that I might be considered for an entry level
marketing position with your company.

Having just graduated from the University of the Mountains with a
B. S. in Business Administration, I am eager to begin my
professional career.  Based upon my experience and qualifications,
summarized in the attached resume, I believe I could make a
valuable contribution to {FIELD}3~.

I can be reached by telephone at 707-555-5665 during working hours.
I would welcome the chance to discuss employment possibilities with
you and would be happy to appear in person for an interview you
might schedule at your convenience.

I look forward to talking with you.

Sincerely,


Harriet Hartley
22 Elm Street
West Washington, NV 89888

Enclosure: Resume
```

**Figure 7-6.**

Insert another field so the address prints on the letter. Place the cursor at the blank line following {FIELD}3~ and enter

| | |
|---|---|
| Shift-F9 | The Merge Codes key, to display the Merge Codes menu |
| 1 | To select the field code |
| 4 | To select field number 4 |

| | |
|---|---|
| ◄┘ | Enter key, to execute the selection |
| ◄┘ | Enter key, to place a blank line after the **{FIELD}4~** line |

**Retrieving a File**

Beginning from the opening WordPerfect screen, retrieve the form letter file by entering,

| | |
|---|---|
| **Shift-F10** | The Retrieve files key. This key can retrieve files more quickly than function key F5. |
| **LETTER.PF** | The filename of the file to be retrieved |
| ◄┘ | Enter key |

**Inserting the Current Date in a Merge**

WordPerfect will insert the computer system's date in a document every time the merge process is used. Rather than typing in a date which has to be continually edited, let WordPerfect insert the date you enter in response to the MS-DOS date prompt.

With the cursor positioned under the first brace in the **{FIELD}1~** code, press

| | |
|---|---|
| **Shift-F9** | The Merge Codes key, to display the Merge Codes menu |
| **6** | Select from additional codes |
| **D** | To insert a **{DATE}** (**^D**) code, or alternatively, use the Down arrow to highlight this choice |
| ◄┘ | Enter key, to select the date code |
| ◄┘ | Enter key, to insert a blank line between the date code and the Field 1 code |

Simple codes such as the **{DATE}** may also be entered by pressing Control and the code character (e.g., D) simultaneously. This saves one keystroke over entering the Merge Codes menu. However, field codes (e.g., **{FIELD}2~**) cannot be entered in this way, and **{END RECORD}** and **{END FIELD}** are more efficiently entered from Shift-F9 since they are always followed by another code, **[HPg]** and **[HRt]** respectively. Overall it may be simpler to use Shift-F9 for all merge codes.

The Date Code will merge the current date into this position in the document. Current date assumes that the computing system running WordPerfect has been booted up properly so that the current date is known to the system.

**Inserting a Message and a Pause for Keyboard Entry**

WordPerfect can combine information from three sources into a document: the primary file, the secondary file, and the keyboard. Input from the keyboard is entered during the merge process.

Position the cursor under the *I* at the beginning of the first paragraph of the letter, *I am writing . . .* .. Type

| | |
|---|---|
| **In response to your recent advertisement in** | |
| | As a new beginning to the sentence |
| **Space** | Space bar, to prepare for the text to follow |
| **Shift-F9** | The Merge Codes key, to display the Merge Codes menu |
| **6** | Select *More* |
| **I** | Select *{INPUT}message~* |
| ◄┘ | Enter key |

| | |
|---|---|
| **Cite ad source** | As the message to be displayed at this point in the text |
| ◂┘ | Enter key, to insert the date code after the message code. Now the merge will pause at this position and the message *Cite ad source* will be displayed at the bottom of the screen as a prompt. |
| , | To place a comma after the name of the source of the advertisement |
| **Space** | Space bar, to leave a space after the comma |

**Further Personalizing the Body of the Letter**

Since it never hurts to mention the firm to which one is applying in the body of the letter, press the Down Arrow as necessary, to move down to the last line of the second paragraph of the body of the letter.

| | |
|---|---|
| **Backspace** | Ten times to delete the period and words *your firm* |
| **Shift-F9** | The Merge Codes key, to display the Merge Codes menu |
| **1** | To choose the Field code. You are prompted for the Field number. |
| **3** | To select the third field, the company name |
| ◂┘ | Enter key. **{FIELD}3~** is inserted at that point. |
| . | To end the sentence |

Replace the old version of **LETTER.PF** and exit the document with the F7 key. Do not exit WordPerfect.

**Managing Keyboard Entry During Merge**

From a blank WordPerfect screen you are now ready to again merge the two files. Press

| | |
|---|---|
| **Ctrl-F9** | To display the Merge/Sort menu |
| **1** | To display the prompt for the primary file |
| **LETTER.PF** | The name of the primary file |
| ◂┘ | Enter key, to receive the prompt for secondary file |
| **RECORDS.SF** | The name of the secondary file |
| ◂┘ | Enter key, to execute the merge |

The merge pauses after the word *in.* Notice that today's date has been placed at the top of the letter (assuming your system was booted up with the correct date). Also notice that the phrase *Cite ad source,* the prompt you inserted at this point in the primary file, appears at the bottom of your screen. Now type

| | |
|---|---|
| **Career Chronicle** | As the fictitious name of the publication where the advertisement is said to have appeared |
| **F9** | The Merge key, to continue the merge after the insertion. Note that at pauses for keyboard entry, the Merge key continues the merge, whereas the Merge/Sort key (Ctrl-F9) can be used to halt the merge at any point. The merge continues in this case, automatically inserting the firm name at the end of the second paragraph, through the end of the first letter and into the second, pausing again for keyboard entry. Type |

**Headhunter's Digest**
As the advertisement source for the second letter

**F9** To continue the merge. The same pause occurs in the third letter.

**West Washington Weekly**
As the advertisement source for the third letter

**F9** To continue the merge, which terminates automatically at the end of the third letter

**Home, Home, ↑** Return to the top of the document

**Grey +** Scroll through the three letters to ensure that all elements of your merge worked successfully. Except for your current date appearing instead of **[today's date]**, the three should look like the portion of the Figure 7-7 shown below:

```
February 15, 1991

Dr. Everett Murchison
Director of Marketing
Collegiate Computing Services
1028 Westport Boulevard
Islandview, California 98765

Dear Dr. Murchison:

In response to your recent advertisement in Career Chronicle, I am
writing in the hope that I might be considered for an entry level
marketing position with your company.

Having just graduated form the University of the Mountains with a
B. S. in Business Administration, I am eager to begin my
professional career.  Based upon my experience and qualifications,
summarized in the attached resume, I believe I could make a
valuable contribution to Collegiate Computing Systems.

I can be reached ...
```

**Figure 7-7.** Portion of Merged Letter

Once you have inspected the three letters and found them correct, print them. You may exit the document without saving it. Return to the beginning WordPerfect screen if you wish to continue. The document could, of course, be saved like any other document, if you wish.

## FURTHER MODIFICATIONS TO THE LETTERS

After the merge has been completed you are free to edit the letters in the file. If you wished to add a paragraph or additional sentences for some letters, you can simply type them in before the file is printed. Similarly, if some sentences need to be modified or deleted, that can be done also.

## OTHER USES OF MERGE

This chapter has introduced you to the merging process. In addition to producing personalized letters, merging can be used for other documents. Merging is used to produce mailing labels, to print addresses on envelopes, telephone lists from secondary files, memorandums, and legal documents in which the text is unchanging but a client's name and other information changes.

## EXERCISES

A. Create a primary file called MEMOHDR.PF which consists of the following text and merge codes:

```
To: {INPUT}Memo to whom? ... Then press F9~

Fr: {INPUT}Memo from whom? ... Then press F9~

Re: {INPUT}Enter the topic/reference ... Then press F9~

Date: {DATE}

{INPUT}Input the memorandum.  Press F9 at the end~
```

Speculate on what purpose for what sort of user this primary file is intended to serve. Next, run a merge with this file; note that no secondary file is needed, since only keyboard entry is required. Finally, critique this primary file's design: what might be done differently?

B. With reference to **RECORDS.SF** as the secondary file, create a primary file called **DAYLIST.PF** which displays the fields of name, title, company, and phone number across the page on a single line. The heading for this list should read like this:

**Resumes sent on {DATE} to the following executives:**

Follow this with a blank line and headings (the fields noted above would serve) for the listing to appear beneath them in tabular form. Put in a **{NEXT RECORD}** code at the end of each line to force the merge to read the next record without putting in an automatic hard page end. Merge the files to test your design, and make whatever adjustments are necessary.

# Chapter 8

# Use of the Mouse

**Chapter Outline**



## THE PURPOSE OF THIS CHAPTER

This text has been written with the assumption that the persons using it are not using a microcomputer with a mouse attached. Some users do have mouse devices, however. This chapter is intended to provide you with an overview of how the mouse is used so you can make the transition from keyboard-oriented commands to mouse-oriented commands.

## WHAT IS A MOUSE?

A mouse is a handheld device that allows a computer user to speed up word processing operations such as:

1. identifying blocks of text that are to be moved or copied,
2. selecting choices from a mouse-oriented series of pop-up menus,
3. moving and scrolling the cursor.

Mouse devices are also used heavily for graphics operations in other types of programs. There are two types of mouse devices available: two button and three button. These are pictured in Figure 8-1a and Figure 8-1b. One type of mouse senses its movement by a roller that moves over any flat surface. Other mouse devices generate light that reflects off of a special tablet with grid markings. The detection of the grid markings indicates the direction and amount of movement of the mouse. The mouse moves easily on an appropriate surface so avoid applying excessive pressure. The mouse can be lifted off of the surface if necessary and brought back down to a new location without moving the cursor arrow.

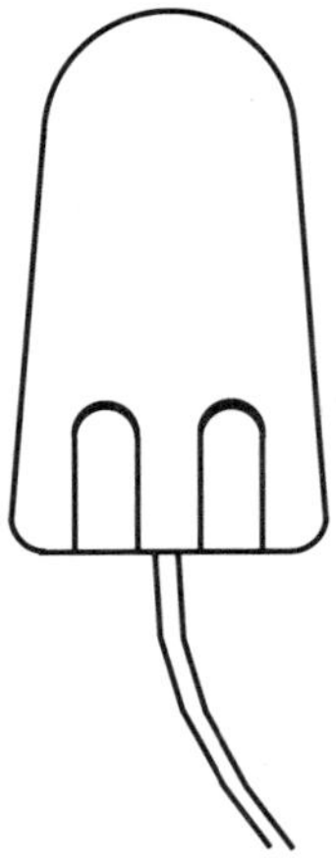

**Figure 8-1a.** A Two-Button Mouse

**Figure 8-1b.** A Three-Button Mouse

## MOUSE OPERATIONS IN WORDPERFECT

Both types of mouse devices can be used with WordPerfect. The mouse creates a block (▮) called a pointer. The pointer does not replace the cursor. The cursor is still visible. The pointer appears when the mouse is activated and disappears when the keyboard is in use. If you move the mouse and the pointer is not visible, continue moving the mouse around until it becomes visible.

| | |
|---|---|
| **Pointing** | The movement of the mouse so that the pointer block (▮) is moved to a new location. |
| **Clicking** | The rapid pressing and releasing of the left button (Enter key). |
| **Canceling** | Pressing the middle button on a three-button mouse; clicking the right button to obtain the menu bar and clicking the right button a second time; pressing the F1 (Cancel) key. |
| **Dragging** | Holding a button down while moving the mouse pointer. |
| **Exiting** | Pressing the right button, when a menu or some prompts are in view, is equivalent to pressing the Exit key (F7). |
| **<choice>** | A notation used in this chapter to request that the pointer block be placed on a menu selection or object before activating a command. |

For either type of mouse, pressing the left button acts the same as the Enter key. The button on the right is the same as the Escape key. For any operation that requires Enter or Escape, one can press the mouse buttons or the keys on the keyboard.

## SAMPLE OPERATIONS

### The Menu Bar

The menu shown in Figure 8-2 can be brought to the top of the work screen by pressing the right button. The pointer can be moved from the document into the menu bar. A pop-up menu for a highlighted menu choice can be brought into view by moving the pointer to the desired choice and pressing the left button (Click(L)). A choice from the pop-up menu can be made by moving the pointer up and down, to select the needed choice. Then click the left button (Click(L)) on the choice. The menu bar can be removed from view at any time by pressing the right button.

```
File Edit Search Layout Mark Tools Font Graphics Help
```

**Figure 8-2.** The Menu Bar

See the menu bar by pressing

| | |
|---|---|
| **Click(R)** | Click the right button, to see the menu bar as shown in Figure 8-2 |
| **Click(R)** | Click the right button a second time, to remove the menu bar |

You will see shortly how you can make selections from the menu bar.

### Scrolling

The pointer can be moved around inside of the document window. Normally, the pointer cannot be moved out of the current window. The right button when depressed, however, allows you to move the cursor beyond to the bottom or top of the screen. Continued depression of this button and "pushing" up against the edge scrolls the text in the document into view.

The mouse does not scroll left or right of the margins, above or below the top or bottom of the document. Although the mouse may place the pointer in an area of the document where there are no characters or embedded codes, when text is blocked, the pointer moves to the closest text.

### Responding to Prompts

Prompts such as "Save file?: Yes (No)" permit use of the mouse to place the pointer on the desired choice and to select the choice by pressing the left button (Click).

### Using the Keyboard

Keyboard commands can be interspersed with mouse-originated commands.

### Blocking

The primary use for a mouse in edit mode is to block text and then to move, delete, or copy that text. The mouse replaces the use of the arrow keys. The arrow keys may take considerably more time to use than the mouse does. Using keyboard commands, retrieve a document of your choice for practice in this lesson. When the document is in view, move the mouse to obtain the pointer. Place the pointer at the beginning of a paragraph and enter

| | |
|---|---|
| **Drag(L)** | Press the left button and hold it down to set blocking on. A prompt to this effect appears in the lower left of the screen. |
| **Move** | Move the pointer with the mouse to place the pointer at the right-most character in the last line of the text to be moved, highlighting the text as the pointer is moved |
| **Release** | Release the left button, to stop blocking |
| **Click(L)** | Click the left button, to remove blocking |

Blocking is used later in this lesson.

**Moving the Cursor**

The cursor and the mouse pointer block are different. The pointer block can be used to move the cursor to a new location, however. Move the pointer with the mouse to any location other than one at which the cursor is located.

| | |
|---|---|
| **Click(L)** | Click the left button a second time. The cursor moves to the location of the pointer block. |

**Blocking Operations**

Blocking can be used to move, copy, and delete text. Try moving some text by placing the pointer at the beginning of a paragraph and entering

| | |
|---|---|
| **Drag(L)** | Click the left button and hold it down to set blocking on. A prompt to this effect appears in the lower left of the screen. |
| **Move** | Move the pointer with the mouse, to place the pointer at the right-most character in the last line of the text to be moved. |
| **Release** | Release the left button, to stop blocking |
| **Click(R)** | Click the right button, to call up the menu bar |
| **<Edit>** | Move the pointer onto Edit |
| **Click(L)** | Click the left button, to bring the pop-up menu for Edit into view |
| **<Delete>** | Move the pointer down with the mouse, to highlight Delete |
| **Click(L)** | Click the left button, to activate Delete. A prompt, "Delete Block? No (Yes)" appears. |
| **<Yes>** | Move the pointer block onto "Yes" |
| **Click(L)** | Select "Yes." The text is deleted. |

This technique is equally applicable to moving and copying text. Moving is shown next. Practice copying on your own.

**Moving**

Moving text is another block operation that illustrates how the mouse can be used to replicate keyboard operations.

| | |
|---|---|
| **Drag(L)** | Depress the left button. Blocking is toggled on. Move the mouse, continuing to hold down the left button, to the last character in the paragraph. |
| **Release** | Free the left button. The text remains blocked. |
| **Click(R)** | Click the right button, to call up the menu bar |
| **<Edit>** | Select Edit |

**Click(L)** Click the left button, to call up the pop-up menu
**<Move>** Select the Move option
**Click(L)** The blocked text is cut from the document. The prompt "Move the cursor; **Press Enter** to retrieve" appears.
**Move ↑↓** Move the pointer block to a new location
**↵** Enter key, to bring the text back to a new location

**File**

Other menus can be recalled and activated in a manner similar to that shown for deletion. Examine one of the pop-up menus more closely. Continue by entering

**Click(R)** Click the right button, to toggle the menu bar on
**<Edit>** Move the pointer to highlight Edit on the menu bar
**Drag(L)** Depress the left button
**Move → ←** Roll the mouse left and right, keeping the pointer inside of the menu bar, to see the pop-up menus associated with each menu choice
**<File>** Stop the pointer on File
**Click(L)** Click the left button, to select File and to view the pop-up menu shown in Figure 8-3

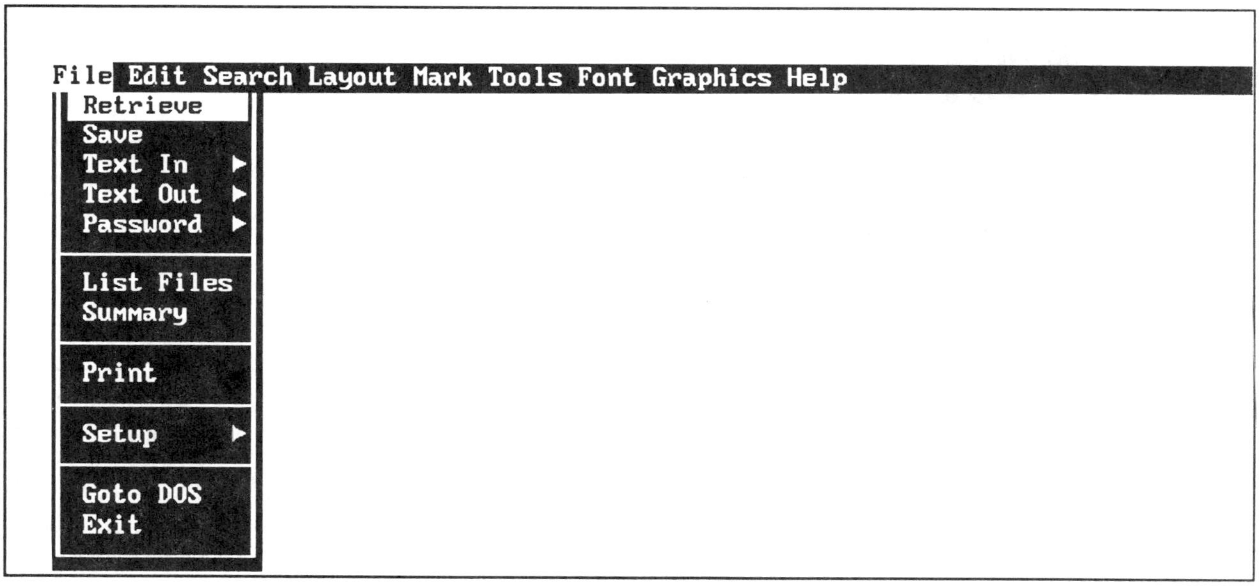


**Figure 8-3.** File Pop-up Menu

**Move ↓↑** Roll the mouse up and down to highlight the choices on the pop-up menu
**<List Files>** Highlight the choice List Files
**Click(L)** Click the left button, to select List Files. The prompt for showing a directory listing appears. Change this directory if necessary.
**Click(R)** Click the right button, to see the files available to choose from in the current directory
**Drag(L)** Depress the left button, to highlight filenames. By moving the pointer to different filenames, they can be selected for menu choice activities.
**<filename>** Highlight any filename of your choice

| | |
|---|---|
| **Move ↓↑** | Move the pointer block out of the highlighted filename down to the menu area |
| **<6 Look>** | Select the Look option |
| **Click(L)** | Click the left button, to view the first page of the document |
| **Click(R)** | Click the right button, to stop looking at the document |
| **Click(R)** | Click the right button, to exit |

**Edit**

The Edit pop-up menu is shown in Figure 8-4. The choices are many of the same as available with the F3 and F4 key operations.

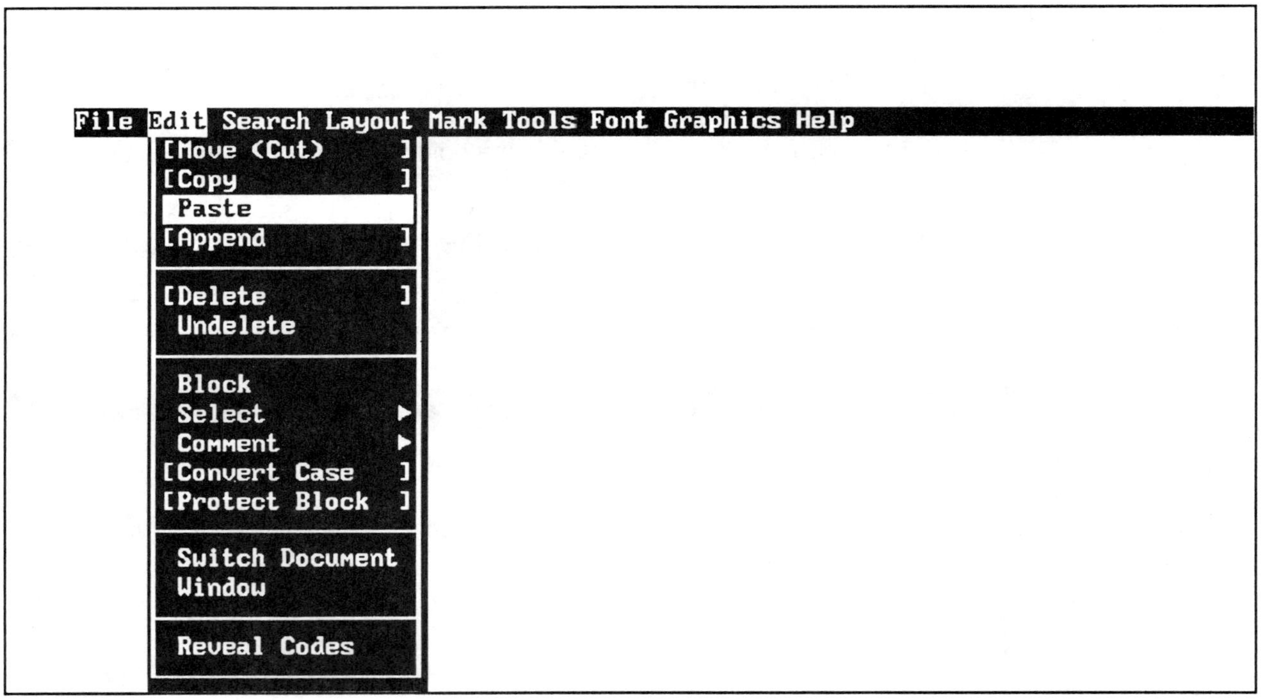


**Figure 8-4.** Edit Pop-up Menu

| | |
|---|---|
| **Click(R)** | Call up the menu bar |
| **<Edit>** | Highlight Edit with the mouse pointer |
| **Click(L)** | Click the left button to select Edit |
| **Drag(L)** | |
| **Move ↓↑** | Roll the mouse up and down to highlight the choices |
| **<Window>** | Highlight the choice Window |
| **Click(L)** | Click the left button to select Window |
| **12** | Type *12* to select the window size |
| **Click(R)** | Click the right button, to complete the operation. Now you are able to view documents 1 and 2 concurrently. |

Follow the same steps to reset the window to twenty-four lines.

## Search

The Search pop-up menu is shown in Figure 8-5. The choices are the same as those that are available with the Search key (F2).

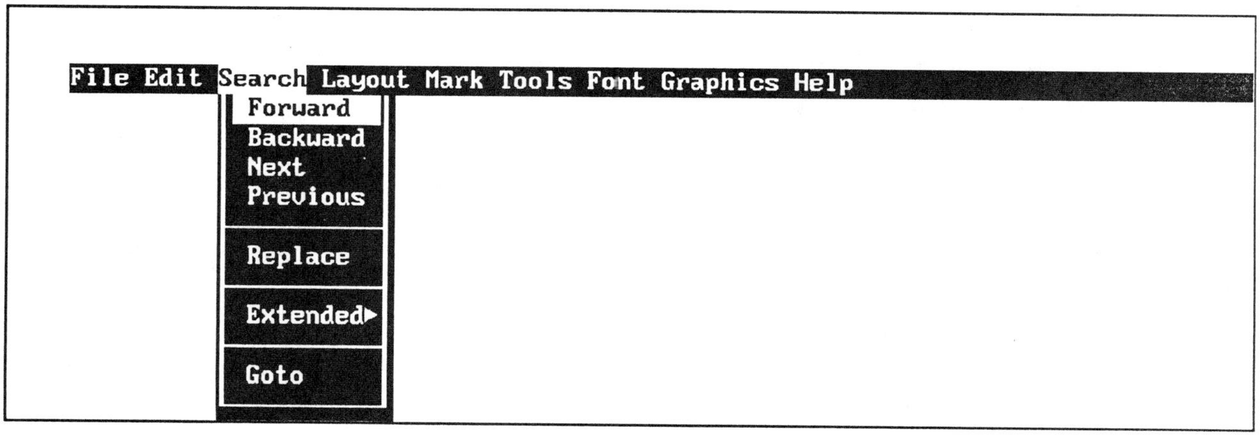


**Figure 8-5.** Search Pop-up Menu

| | |
|---|---|
| **Click(R)** | Click the right button to call up the menu bar |
| **<Search>** | Highlight the Search option |
| **Click(L)** | Click the left button, to select the Search option and view the Search menu |
| **Move ↓↑** | Roll the mouse to the choice *Forward* |
| **Click(L)** | Click the left button to select *Forward.* You are prompted to enter a word at the "-> Srch:" prompt |
| **the** | With spaces on both sides, enter the word *the* or any word that is contained in your document |
| **Click(R)** | Click the right button to complete the operation and to have the cursor moved to the first instance of the word in your document |

Other types of searches can be carried out in a very similar fashion.

## Layout

The Layout pop-up menu is shown in Figure 8-6. The choices are many of the same as those available with the F7 and F8 key operations. Enter the following:

| | |
|---|---|
| **Click(R)** | Click the right button to obtain the menu bar |
| **<Layout>** | Highlight the Layout option |
| **Click(L)** | Click the left button to select the layout option |
| **Move ↓↑** | Roll the mouse pointer |
| **<Align>** | Select *Align* |
| **Click(L)** | Click the left button, to call another pop-up menu associated with Align |
| **Move ↓↑** | Roll mouse cursor |
| **<Hard Page>** | Select *Hard Page,* to enter a hard page code |
| **Click(L)** | Click the left mouse key, to enter the code |

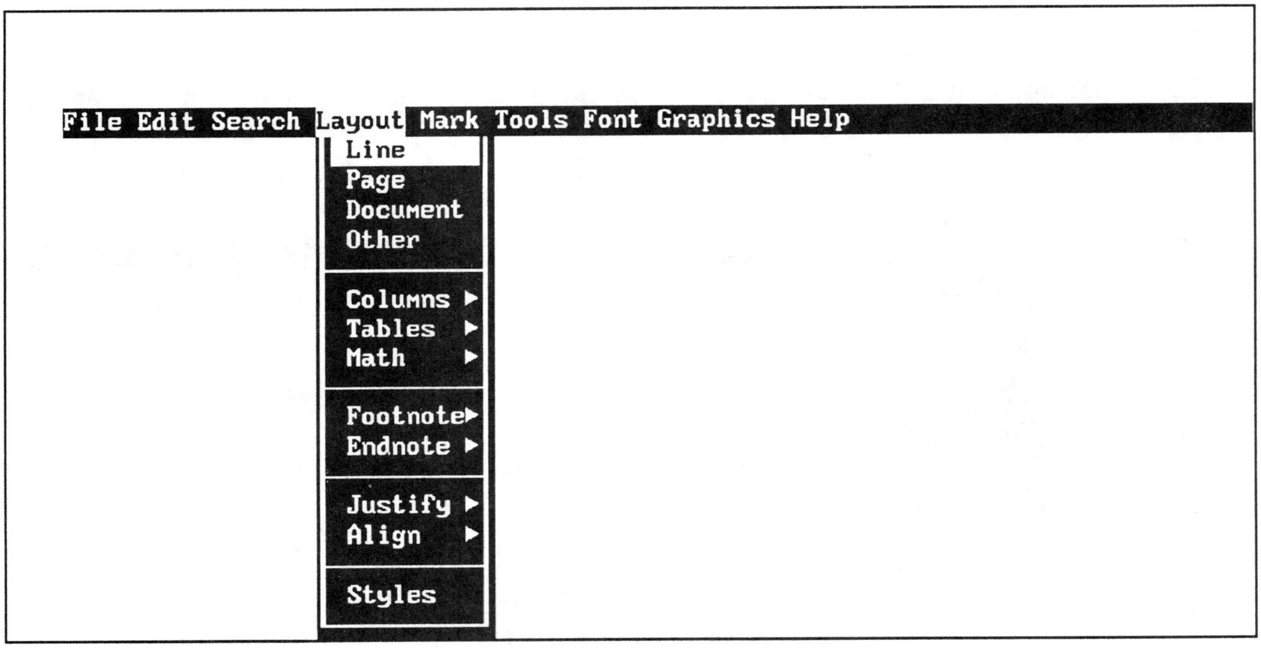


**Figure 8-6.** Layout Pop-up Menu

### Mark

The Mark pop-up menu is shown in Figure 8-7. The choices are the same as those that are available with the F5 key options.

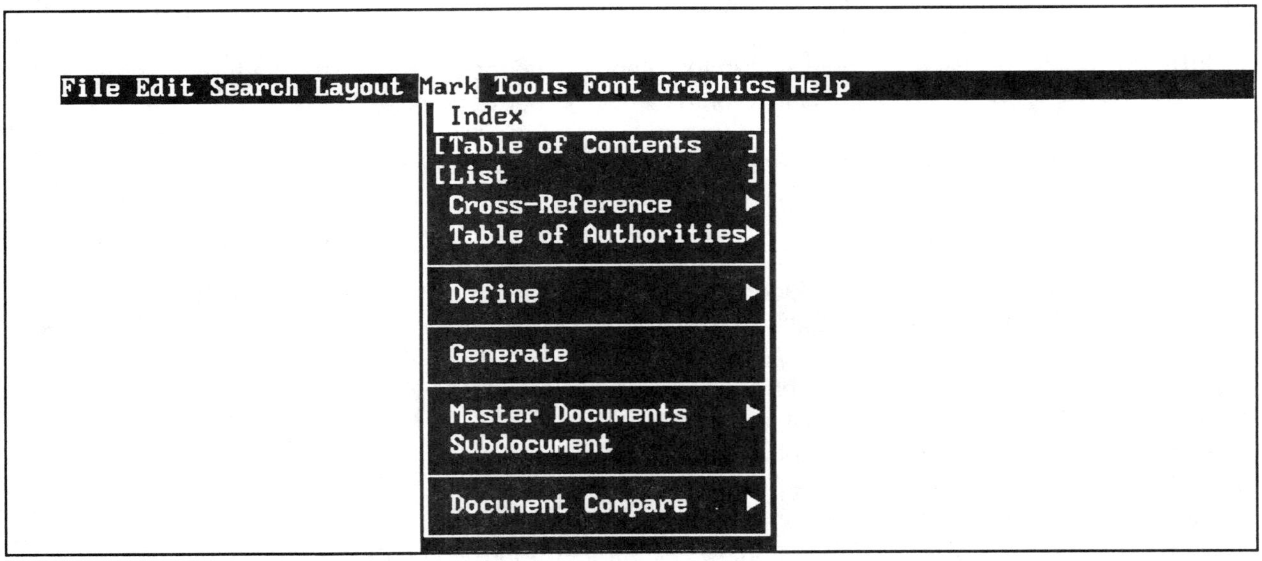


**Figure 8-7.** Mark Pop-up Menu

**Tools**

The Tools pop-up menu is shown in Figure 8-8. The choices are many of the same as available with the Alt-F1 (Thesaurus), Ctrl-F2 (Spell), Ctrl-F3 (Line Draw), F9 (Merge/Sort, Merge codes) Alt-F10 (Macro) keys.

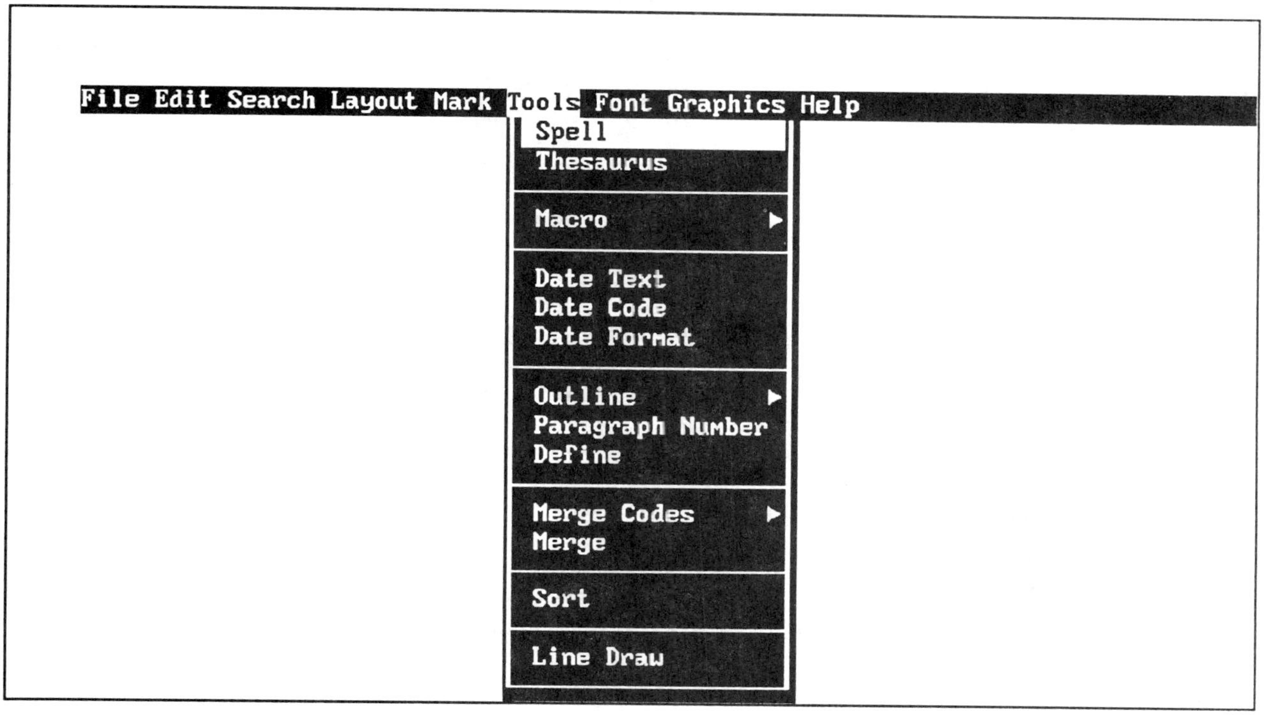


**Figure 8-8.** Tools Pop-up Menu

| | |
|---|---|
| **Click(R)** | Click the right button, to obtain the menu bar |
| **<Tools>** | Highlight Tools |
| **Click(L)** | Click the left button, to select Tools |
| **Move ↓↑** | Move pointer to the selection Spell |
| **Click(L)** | Click left mouse button to select the Spell option |
| **Move ↓↑** | Move mouse pointer to the bottom of the screen and highlight **2** Page, to have spelling checker review the page for spelling errors |
| **Click(L)** | Click the left button, to select and initiate the Page spell check. If any words are highlighted by the spelling checker, use the mouse to make selections from the Spell menu by clicking the left button or pressing function key F1 to cancel. |

**Font**

The Font pop-up menu is shown in Figure 8-9. The choices are the same as those that are available with the F3 and the F8 keys.

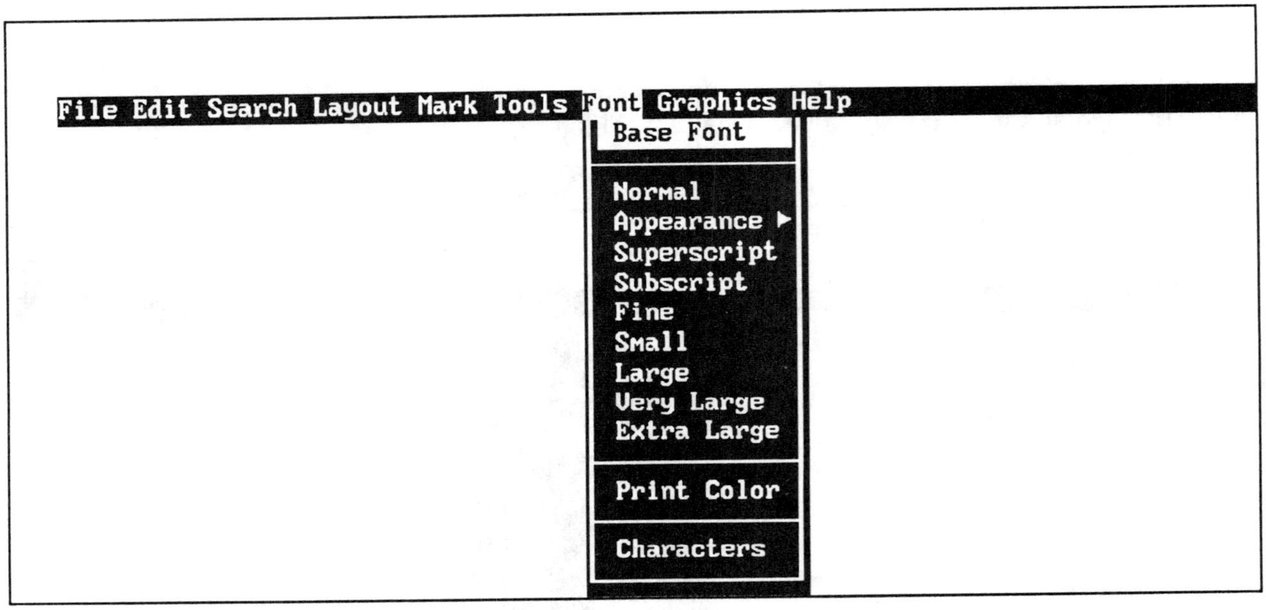


**Figure 8-9.** Font Pop-up Menu

Place the cursor at the beginning of a line and enter

| | |
|---|---|
| Click(L) | Click the left button and hold it down, to set blocking on. A prompt to this effect appears in the lower left of the screen. |
| Drag(L) | Move the pointer with the mouse to place the pointer at the right-most character in the line, highlighting the text as the pointer is moved |
| Release | Release the left button to stop blocking |

Underline the blocked text by entering

| | |
|---|---|
| Click(R) | Click the right button to obtain the menu bar |
| <Font> | Highlight the option Font |
| Click(L) | Click the left button, to select Font |
| Move ↓↑ | Roll the mouse pointer |
| <Appearance> | Highlight Appearance to alter the appearance of the text you will type shortly |
| Click(L) | Click the left button, to select Appearance |
| <Underline> | Highlight Underline |
| Click(L) | Click the left button, to select the underlining option. The text is underlined and shows a different background color. |

### Graphics

The Graphics pop-up menu is shown in Figure 8-10. The choices are the same as those that are available with the Alt-F9 key (Graphics).

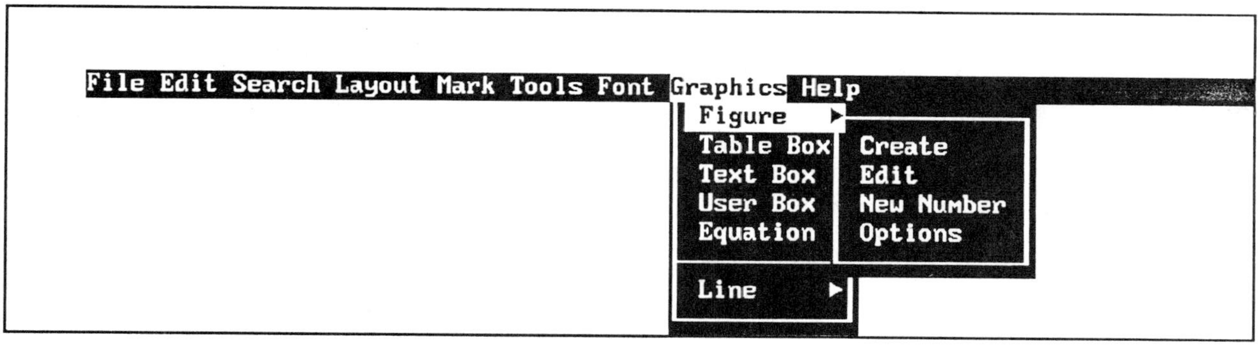


**Figure 8-10.** Graphics Pop-up Menu

**Help**

The Help pop-up menu is shown in Figure 8-11. The choices are the same as those that are available with the F3 key (Help).

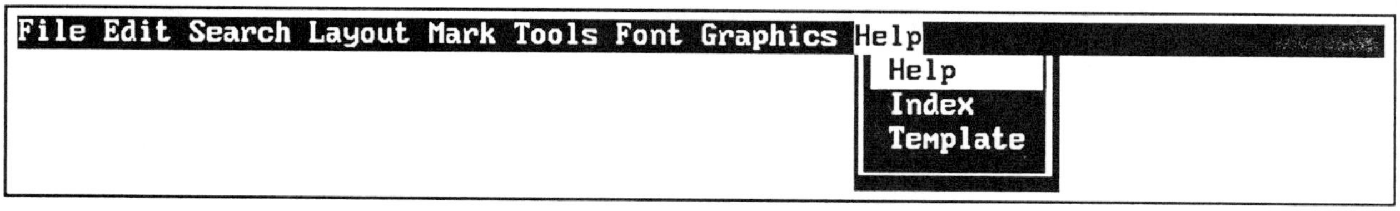


**Figure 8-11.** Help Pop-up Menu

| | |
|---|---|
| **Click(R)** | Click right button to obtain the menu bar |
| **<help>** | Highlight Help selection |
| **Click(L)** | Click the left button, to select Help |
| **Move ↓↑** | Roll pointer to Template |
| **Click(L)** | Click the left button to select Template, to view the Help template that would ordinarily go over the function keys on the keyboard |
| **Click(R)** | Click the right button, to cancel the Help template and return to document |

**Windowing**

Control-F3 can be used to split the screen so you can see two documents. When the screen is split, the mouse can move the pointer from one window to the other.

## EXITING

Documents can be exited using a mouse, also. To exit the document you are in, press

| | |
|---|---|
| **Click(R)** | Click the right button to obtain the menu bar |
| **<File>** | Highlight the file option |
| **Click(L)** | Click the left button to call up the File pop-up menu |
| **Move ↓↑** | Move the pointer to the selection Exit |
| **Click(L)** | Click the left button, to select the exit option. The R.S.V.P prompt asking whether you wish to save the document appears. |

| | |
|---|---|
| **Move ↓↑** | Move the mouse pointer to make the selection |
| **Click(L)** | Click left button on **No** if you do not want to save these few changes, otherwise click on **Yes** |
| **Click(L)** | Press left button on **No** to continue working in WordPerfect or on **Yes** to quit. |

## INTERPRETING KEYBOARD COMMANDS

One of the operations that was discussed earlier in this chapter was the movement of text as a block operation. This operation illustrates how the mouse can be used to replicate keyboard operations.

| MOUSE COMMAND | ACTION | KEYBOARD COMMAND |
|---|---|---|
| **Drag(L)** | Start blocking the text to be moved | **Alt-F4** |
| **Move** | Move the cursor (pointer) to the end of the block | **Arrow keys** |
| **Release** | Stop blocking | |
| **Click(R)** | Call up the menu bar | **Ctrl-F4** |
| **<Edit>** | Select Edit | **Move: 1 Block** |
| **Click(L)** | Activate Edit | |
| **<Move>** | Select Move | **1 Move;** |
| **Click(L)** | Cut text | |
| **Move** | Move the cursor to the "move to" location | **Arrow keys** |
| ◄┘ | Enter the text at the location of the cursor | ◄┘ |

## SUMMARY

Many software programs are being designed to take advantage of mouse capabilities. Initially, it takes time to practice using the mouse enough to gain a comfortable familiarity with mouse-oriented commands. After this initial period of adjustment, you will find that using a mouse can make many operations seem more natural and efficient. The effort involved is worth your time.

# Appendix

## Function Key/Menu/Screen Summary

**F1 Cancel/Undo**
- Restore
- Previous Deletion

**F2 Forward Search**
**F3 Help**
**F4 Indent**
**F5 List Files**
- Retrieve
- Delete
- Move/Rename
- Print
- Short/Long Display
- Look
- Other Directory
- Copy
- Find
  - Name
  - Document Summary
  - First Page
  - Entire Document
  - Conditions
  - Undo
- Name Search

**F6 Bold**
**F7 Exit**
**F8 Underline**
**F9 End Field**
**F10 Save**
**F11 Reveal Codes**
**F12 Block**
**Shift-F1 Setup**
- Mouse
  - Type
  - Port
  - Double Click Interval
  - Submenu Delay Time
  - Accelerator Factor
  - Left-handed Mouse
  - Assisted Mouse Pointer
- Display
  - Colors/Fonts/Attributes
  - Graphics Screen Type
  - Text Screen Type
  - Menu Options
  - View-Document Options
  - Edit-Screen Options
- Environment
  - Backup Options
  - Beep Options
  - Cursor Speed
  - Document Management/Summary
  - Fast Save
  - Hyphenation
  - Prompt for Hyphenation
  - Units of Measure
- Initial Settings
  - Merge
  - Date Format
  - Equations
  - Format Retrieved Documents for Default Printer
  - Initial Codes
  - Repeat Value
  - Table of Authorities
  - Print Options
- Keyboard Layout
  - ALTRNAT
  - ENHANCED
  - EQUATION
  - MACROS
  - SHORTCUT
- Location of Files
  - Backup Files
  - Keyboard/Macro Files
  - Thesaurus/Spell/Hyphenation
    - Main
    - Supplementary
  - Printer Files
  - Style Files
    - Library Filename
  - Graphic Files
  - Documents

**Shift-F2 Reverse Search**
**Shift-F3 Switch**
**Shift-F4 Indent Left/Right**

**Shift-F5 Date/Outline**
- Date Text
- Date Code
- Date Format
- Outline
  - On
  - Off
  - Move Family
  - Copy Family
  - Delete Family
- Para Num
- Define
  - Starting Paragraph Number
  - Paragraph
  - Outline
  - Legal
  - Bullets
  - User-Defined
  - Enter Inserts Paragraph Number
  - Automatically Adjust to Current Level
  - Outline Style Name

**Shift-F6 Center**

**Shift-F7 Print**
- Print
  - Full Document
  - Page
  - Document on Disk
  - Control Printer
  - Multiple Pages
  - View Document
  - Initialize Printer
- Options
  - Select Printer
  - Binding Offset
  - Number of Copies
  - Multiple Copies Generated By
  - Graphics Quality
  - Text Quality

**Shift-F8 Format**
- Line
  - Hyphenation
  - Hyphenation Zone
  - Justification
  - Line Height
  - Line Numbering
  - Line Spacing
  - Margins (Left/Right)
  - Tab Set
  - Widow/Orphan Protection
- Page
  - Center Page
  - Force Odd/Even Pages
  - Headers
  - Footers
  - Margins (Top/Bottom)
  - Page Numbering
  - Paper (Size/Type)
  - Suppress
- Document
  - Display Pitch
  - Initial Codes
  - Initial Base Font
  - Redline Method
  - Summary
- Other
  - Advance
  - Conditional End of Page
  - Decimal/Align Character
  - Thousands' Separator
  - Language
  - Overstrike
  - Printer Functions
  - Underline (Spaces/Tabs)
  - Border Options

**Shift-F9 Merge Codes**
- Field
- End Record
- Input
- Page Off
- Next Record
- More

**Shift-F10 Retrieve**

**Alt-F1 Thesaurus**
- Replace Word
- View Document
- Look Up Word
- Clear Column

**Alt-F2 Search and Replace**

**Alt-F3 Reveal Codes**

**Alt-F4 Block**

**Alt-F5 Mark Text**
- Cross-Ref
- Subdoc
- Index
- ToA Short Form
- Define
- Generate

**Alt-F6 Flush Right**
**Alt-F7 Columns/Table**
- Columns
  - On
  - Off
  - Define
- Tables
  - Create
  - Edit
- Math
  - On
  - Off
  - Define
  - Calculate

**Alt-F8 Style**
- On
- Off
- Create
- Edit
- Delete
- Save
- Retrieve
- Update

**Alt-F9 Graphics**
- Figure
- Table Box
- Text Box
- User Box
- Line
- Equation

**Alt-F10 Macro**
**Ctrl-F1 DOS Shell**
- Go to DOS
- DOS Command

**Ctrl-F2 Spell**
- Word
- Page
- Document
- New Supplementary Dictionary
- Look Up
- Count

**Ctrl-F3 Screen**
- Window
- Line Draw
- Rewrite

**Ctrl-F4 Move/Copy**
- (Blocking Off)
  - Sentence
  - Paragraph
  - Page
  - Retrieve
- (Blocking On)
  - Block
  - Tabular Column
  - Rectangle

**Ctrl-F5 Text In/Out**
- DOS Text
- Password
- Save As
- Comment
- Spreadsheet

**Ctrl-F6 Tab Align**
**Ctrl-F7 Footnote**
- Footnote
- Endnote
- Endnote Placement

**Ctrl-F8 Font**
- Size
  - Superscript
  - Subscript
  - Fine
  - Small
  - Large
  - Very Large
  - Extra Large
- Appearance
  - Bold
  - Underline
  - Double Underline
  - Italic
  - Outline
  - Shadow
  - Small Cap
  - Redline
  - Strikeout
- Normal
- Base Font
  - Select
  - Name Search
- Print Color

**Ctrl-F9 Merge/Sort**
- Merge
- Sort
- Convert Old Merge Codes

**Ctrl-F10 Macro Definition**

# Glossary

. Symbolic representation for the current directory.

.. Symbolic representation of the parent directory of the current directory.

* The DOS and WordPerfect wild card for matching multiple characters in command line parameters.

\ Symbolic representation for the root directory.

A

**A>** The DOS system prompt signifying drive A as the default drive.

**Active document** The document, 1 or 2, in which the cursor is currently positioned.

**Alignment** The placement of text on a line.

**Alphabetic keys** The keys on the computer's keyboard that are arranged just as they are on a typewriter keyboard.

**Alphanumeric characters** Any combination of letters, numbers, symbols, and spaces.

**Alternate key** The key marked Alt and used to attach alternate meanings to other alphanumeric keys in WordPerfect.

**Application** The product of a generalized application program such as a document from a word processor, a budget projection from a spreadsheet, or an inventory from a database manager.

**Application program** A program that allows users to produce specific applications of the computer to a particular area or need.

**ASCII** American Standard Code for Information Interchange; the coding scheme whereby every character, number, or symbol is represented by an integer code between 0 and 255.

**ASCII files** Text files saved in a format specified by the American Standard Code for Information Interchange. Files saved in this format often can be used by other programs, or transmitted by modem because they have a standard format.

**Automatic repeat** The characteristic of keys, if held down, to continue to enter the symbol they represent after the first entry of the character and a brief pause.

**Auxiliary files** Files that an application program uses to supplement the main program files.

B

**B>** The DOS system prompt signifying drive B as the default drive.

**Back up** A process of making a second copy of a file to avoid loss of data. Backups may be created automatically by some applications programs.

**Backup copy** A duplicate of a file or disk that is saved in case the original file or disk is damaged.

**Bad sector** A disk sector that has been damaged and marked as unusable by DOS.

**Beep** An audible sound notifying a user of an error.

**Binding width** The addition of extra space in the left margin for odd-numbered pages and in the right margin for even-numbered pages to allow space for a binding mechanism.

**Block** In WordPerfect, a highlighted block of text that is to be copied, moved, or otherwise manipulated. Also, a contiguous character string.

**Block protect** In WordPerfect, a pair of codes that prevents the intervening text from being divided by a soft page break.

**Block text** In WordPerfect, the process of highlighting text with the Move key (Ctrl-F4).

**Bold text** Text that is darker or "brighter" than normal text.

**Boot** To load and run the operating system. Derived from "pull yourself up by your own bootstraps."

**Byte** A unit of representation constructed from eight bits. A byte represents a single character.

C **C>** The DOS system prompt signifying drive C, the hard drive, as the default drive.

**Cancel** To abort a program or command.

**Carriage return (CR)** A printer directive moving the print head down one line and back to the left margin. Issued by pressing the Enter (Return) key on most programs.

**Case** The shape and size of a letter. Letters in a type style may be uppercase or lowercase.

**Case sensitive** A command that acts differently if characters are typed in lowercase or uppercase.

**Center** In WordPerfect, the use of the Center key (Shift-F6) to position a word or phrase between the current margins.

**Center indent** A WordPerfect code (Shift-F4) that temporarily indents text equally from the right and left margins.

**Center page** A WordPerfect code that places text on a page with equal top and bottom margins.

**Character** A symbol (numeric, alphabetic, punctuation, or mathematic) represented by one byte.

**Character string** See String.

**Code** A symbol embedded in the text of a document that affects the formatting or printing of the text.

**Cold boot** Starting the computer by turning it on.

**Color display** A monitor that displays color.

**Color/Graphics Monitor Adapter** The printed-circuit card for personal computers that provides low-level graphics and minimal colors.

**Command** An instruction to a computer that can be executed.

**Commercial software** Software that has been copyrighted and licensed, is supported by the developer, and that must be paid for in advance of its usage.

**Compressed type** Small type size. For example, a type size of 17.5 cpi. A typical size is 10 or 12 cpi.

**Condensed type** See Compressed type.

**Configuration** The currently active default values for an operating system or for an applications program. These values may be modifiable during operation.

**Control code** A code entered by pressing the Control key and another key at the same time. The caret, ^, often symbolizes the Control key. Control keys permit the issuance of DOS commands for disparate activities such as rebooting, aborting a program, and suspending program execution. In WordPerfect, Control codes insert formatting codes.

**cpi** Characters per inch.

**CPU** Central processing unit. The unit that processes data and supports random access memory (RAM).

**Current directory** The default DOS directory. The directory that is employed first when DOS searches for files and executable commands unless otherwise directed.

**Current drive** The drive containing the disk on which DOS looks for a directory or file unless otherwise instructed.

**Cursor** The underscore character that indicates where characters will be entered or where commands will be carried out.

D **Data disk** The disk used to store files.

**Database** An organized collection of related records containing data suitable for manipulation by a database program.

**Database field** One element in a database structure that is defined by a field name, a length, and a type.

**Database record** The fields that compose an entry in a database.

**Debug** To discover and correct syntactic and semantic errors in a program, function, macro, batch file, or subroutine.

**Decimal tab** A tab marker for which numbers are centered on a period.

**Default directory** See Current directory.

**Default drive** See Current drive.

**Default value** The value used or the action taken when an acceptable alternative has not been specified.

**Desktop Publishing** A software package that integrates graph and text materials suitable for high quality publications.

**Destination** The target location for data or files transferred from a source location.

**Dir** In DOS, the command for listing the names of files and directories.

**Directory** A logical grouping of files and subdirectories on a disk. A directory's filenames, extensions, and subdirectory names are displayed together along with the file's size, creation time, and date.

**Directory hierarchy** The treelike, logical structure holding subdirectories. Subdirectories of root have subdirectories created under them, and so on.

**Disk drive** The device that reads and writes files to disks.

**Diskette** A secondary storage medium for a computer. Diskettes come in floppy, rigid, and semirigid cases.

**Display** The monitor screen. Also, in dBASE, a command for listing the contents of records.

**Doc number** In WordPerfect, the number of the document the cursor is located in. Two documents may be in use simultaneously.

**DOS** Disk Operating System. The software that makes computer hardware usable.

**Dot leader tab** A tab marker that fills the space up to tabbed text with dots rather than blank space.

**Double-density disk** A disk with 360 Kb of storage.

**Double sided** A diskette with two surfaces on which to store files.

**Drive name** The characters (a letter and a colon) that identify a disk drive. Examples include *C:* and *A:*.

E

**Edit** To check or modify documents, worksheets, data, or program codes.

**Embedded code** A word processing code that affects the formatting but not the contents of the document.

**Empty directory** A directory that has no subdirectories or files beneath it.

**Endnote** A reference or citation that appears at the end of a document.

**Enter key** Synonymous with Return key. Represented by a broken arrow on some keyboards. The Enter key inserts a carriage return and a line feed.

**Error message** A warning that a command cannot be performed as requested.

**Escape key** The key used to back out of some command sequences in WordPerfect, to cancel a command in DOS, and to indicate the number of times commands should be executed in WordPerfect.

**Extension** Up to three characters that are added to a filename to identify the contents of the file.

F

**File** A collection of data stored in a named and dedicated portion of a disk. Files can contain graphs, documents, databases, worksheets, programs, and other collections of data.

**File specification** The complete specification of a file including a drive letter, a pathway, a filename, and an extension. Also, abbreviated to filespec.

**Filename** The identifier that uniquely describes a file. Consists of from one to eight characters.

**Floppy disk** Diskettes that allow some physical flexibility, especially of the 3 1/2" and 5 1/4" size.

**Flush right** In WordPerfect, to force text to align with the right margin.

**Font** A typeface such as elite, Gothic Roman, or italics.

**Footnote** A reference or citation that appears at the bottom of a page.

**Form feed (FF)** A printer control character that advances the paper to the next sheet.

**Formatting** Initializing and preparing a disk so that it can record and store files produced by a particular computer system. Also, the appearance of text in a document or worksheet.

**Formatting code** See Embedded code.

**Function keys** Keys marked F1 through F10 (or F12) that carry out specialized macro operations in DOS and in applications software.

G

**Global search-and-replace** The ability to locate and modify all instances of a character string or value found in a worksheet, document, database, or other file.

**Graphics** The use of images in an applications program.

H

**Hanging indent** In WordPerfect, the temporary indentation (movement of the left margin) of a paragraph with the Indent (F4) key. The indentation terminates with the first hard return.

**Hard disk** Secondary storage device with a rigid disk.

**Hard font** A font built into a printer or provided on a font cartridge that is inserted into a printer.

**Hard hyphen** A hyphen inserted in a WordPerfect document when you press the hyphen key.

**Hard page break** In WordPerfect, a code inserted with Ctrl-Enter to force the printer to move to the next sheet. Hard page breaks are not adjusted if text that is added or deleted expands or reduces the number of lines on the page.

**Hard return** In WordPerfect, a code inserted when the Enter (Return) key is pressed. Indicates that the line should be broken at that point and that words should not be filled from below if text above the code is deleted.

**Hard space** In WordPerfect, a space entered with Home-Space Bar to keep two words together on a line.

**Help** An on-line program for providing assistance.

**Help key** The key that recalls Help screens (F3 in WordPerfect).

**High density disk** See Quad-density disk.

**Home key** The key that, in association with directional arrows, moves the cursor in WordPerfect.

**Hot zone** An adjustable area to the left of the right margin in a document. Words beginning to the left of the hot zone and extending beyond the margin are hyphenated.

**Hyphenation** The division of words that extend across the hot zone into two parts, one part on each of two lines, divided by a hyphen. Hyphenation can be toggled on and off.

I

**IBM-compatible computer** A computer capable of executing identically to an IBM computer. Also called a clone.

**Indent** Use of the Tab key to insert a tab code in a WordPerfect document.

**Initialize** To set up a diskette, a program, or a device with default values and conditions.

**Insert mode** A mode of data entry in which new text is inserted into existing text rather than overwriting it. Opposite of overwrite mode.

**Installation** The process of tailoring the default values for an applications program to the hardware available and to the user's priorities for initial program parameters such as screen colors, margins, and so on.

J

**Justification** See Alignment.

K

**Kerning** A way of spacing printed characters so that they are closer together.

**Key field** A field in a secondary file used for sorting.

**Keyboard, extended** 101 keys.

**Keyboard, standard** 80 keys.

L

**Line draw** Use of the Screen key (Ctrl-F3) in WordPerfect to draw single- and double-line boxes in documents.

**Line feed (LF)** A control code that advances the printer head to the next line.

**Line format** That portion of the Format menu that adjusts the default characteristics of a line such as the margins, height, tab ruler, and line spacing.

**List files** The key (F5) in WordPerfect that displays filenames in the default directory and permits their manipulation.

**List of Styles** A group of predefined sets of formatting codes created as a part of a document, or saved as a separate file to be used by all documents of the same type.

**Ln** In WordPerfect, the line the cursor is located on.

**Look** A List Files option that enables the user to see the contents of documents before the document is retrieved.

M

**Margin** The blank space borders at the top, bottom, left, and right of a printed document, worksheet, or database report.

**Margin release** The process of moving the cursor one tab stop to the left of the left margin. Executed with Shift-Tab in WordPerfect.

**Margin setting** A WordPerfect code that specifies the amount of blank space above, below, to the left, and to the right of text.

**Mark Text** The key in WordPerfect used to block text so that it can be moved, copied, indexed, referenced, or otherwise used to insert formatting commands.

**Menu** A series of choices from which the user is to make selections.

**Merge Codes key** In WordPerfect, Shift-F9, used to select and insert a merge code into a document.

**Merge/Sort key** In WordPerfect, Ctrl-F9, used to initiate a merge or sort operation involving a primary and a secondary file.

**Merging** The operation by which data from a data or secondary file are merged with a primary file (a document) to produce a series of unique documents.

**Mixed case** Text containing both uppercase and lowercase characters.

**MS-DOS** Abbreviation for Microsoft-Disk Operating System. The operating system used on IBM PC compatible computers.

N

**Nonproportional spacing** Requires each printed character to occupy the same amount of space.

**Nonsystem disk** A nonbootable diskette. A diskette that does not contain the hidden files and/or the COMMAND.COM file needed to successfully carry out a boot.

**Num Lock key** The key used to toggle the numeric keypad between lowercase and uppercase.

**Numeric keypad** The block of ten keys holding numbers as uppercase and cursor movement keys as lowercase.

O

**Operating System** A program that coordinates the operation of all parts of a computer system.

**Outline** A WordPerfect feature that inserts outlining codes that automatically designate the number and/or letter to identify each level of entry in an outlined list.

**Output device** Any device receiving data from a computer. Common output devices are the monitors, printers, and plotters.

**Overstrike** The printing of one letter in the same space occupied by another letter to produce the new letter.

**Overwrite mode** The mode of data entry in which typed characters type over and replace existing text. Opposite of Insert mode.

P

**Page break** The point at which paper in the printer will be ejected.

**Page format** That portion of the Format key (Shift-F8) in WordPerfect used, for example, to center text on a page, set binding widths, set page numbering, change top and bottom margins, add headers and footers, and change paper size.

**Parent directory** The directory above a subdirectory.

**Path name** A character string that describes the precise order of directories that DOS must traverse in order to locate a file or command. Part of the file specification.

**PC** Abbreviation for personal computer.

**PC-DOS** Abbreviation for Personal Computer - Disk Operating System. The operating system used on IBM personal computers. Comparable to MS-DOS.

**Peripheral device** Devices such as printers and modems connected to the system unit and that communicate through an adapter card.

**Pg** In WordPerfect, the page the cursor is located on.

**Pitch** The number of characters printed per inch. The most frequently used pitches are 10 pitch (pica) and 12 pitch (elite).

**Pos** In WordPerfect, the column in which the cursor is located.

**Primary document** In merge printing, the document that contains the text to be repeated in all copies, as well as the codes that direct the insertion of data from the secondary, or data file.

**Printer control** The WordPerfect command (Shift-F7, C) used to manage the printing of documents. This includes canceling a job, stopping and restarting the printer, and changing a job's priority.

**Printer control codes** Codes that control the operation of the printer. Control codes may change type sizes and styles, send line feeds and page feeds. Printer command codes are often particular to specific printers. Application programs include driver sets that convert user-entered control code symbols to printer control codes designed for a specific printer.

**Program** A sequence of instructions that a computer can execute to accomplish a task.

**Program disk** The disk that contains the main program for an application. Also called a System Disk.

**Prompt** The signal that control has been passed to the user and that the system is awaiting a command or data entry.

**Proportional spacing** The technique of adjusting the space given to characters on a print line to match their width. A *W* is given more space than an *i*.

**Public-domain software** Software that is not copyrighted or supported by the developer.

Q

**Quad-density disk** A disk with 1.2 Mb storage.

**Qwerty keys** The standard arrangement of alphabetic and numeric keys. Derives from the letters on the top left row.

R

**Random Access Memory (RAM)** The portion of the computer's memory that stores the internal DOS commands, programs, and data. Also called main memory or primary memory.

**Read** The process of copying data from a file into RAM.

**Reboot** See Warm boot.

**Record** A single entry in a database. Also the collection of related fields that compose a record structure.

**Reformatting** Re-adjusting text in a document after changes have been made. Also, formatting a disk a second time.

**Retrieve** Load a worksheet into RAM.

**Return key** See Enter key.

**Right-justified tab** A tab marker that places text to the left of the tab.

**Root directory** The first directory on any disk. Root is created during formatting. All other directories are user-created subdirectories of root.

**R.S.V.P.** A WordPerfect request for a yes-or-no response.

**Ruler** A WordPerfect code that specifies the left and right margins.

S

**Save** To write a file to secondary storage.

**Scrolling** The line-by-line movement of data on the monitor.

**Search** The automatic location of a user-entered character string.

**Search-and-replace** The automatic location and replacement of a user-entered character string with another user-entered character string.

**Search string** The user-entered character string which is to be located through a search command.

**Second document** The document seen in the second WordPerfect window.

**Secondary file** A file that stores variable information to be merged into the primary document during a merge printing operation. Also known as a data file.

**Sector** A 512-byte portion of a floppy or hard disk onto which data are written, or read from. Each track is divided into sectors to permit the location of data by a disk address. Also used to describe a single pie-shaped portion of a disk created by formatting.

**Setup** The initial configuration of a program or hardware device.

**Shareware** Software that has been copyrighted but is distributed on a try-it-first basis. Then, if it is useful, the user contributes a recommended amount to the developer.

**Shift-state keys** The Alternate, Control, and Shift keys: keys that change the state of the other keyboard characters.

**Soft font** A font supplied on a floppy disk that can be downloaded to a printer.

**Soft hyphen** A hyphen inserted by WordPerfect through automatic hyphenation.

**Soft page break** In WordPerfect, a code automatically inserted to eject the paper to the next page when the maximum number of lines on a page has been printed. Soft page breaks are adjusted if text that is added or deleted expands or reduces the number of lines on the page.

**Soft return** The code inserted by WordPerfect at the end of a line that is word wrapped. A soft return can be automatically reformatted. Opposite of a hard return.

**Soft space** A normal space entered with the space bar. In WordPerfect, a soft space can be used to break words.

**Software** Programs that are used with a computer system. (In contrast to hardware.)

**Source disk** The disk from which data are read or copied.

**Source file** The file from which data are being read or copied.

**Status line** The bottom line of WordPerfect documents.

**String** One or more connected characters that are used as a unit for some computer operation.

**Styles** Previously defined formats that can be quickly incorporated in documents.

**Styles library** The default list of styles. The Styles Library is designated with the Setup key to serve the most commonly used documents.

**Subdirectory** A directory created beneath another directory.

**Subdocument** In WordPerfect, a document that is used as part of a master document.

**Subscript** A half-sized number or letter placed one-half line beneath the current line.

**Superscript** A half-sized number or letter placed one-half line above the current line.

**Switch** The movement of the cursor between documents.

**System disk** A disk containing the files needed for booting a booting system. Sometimes used to refer to the main program disk for an applications program.

T

**Tab indent** See Indent.

**Tab-Left indent** A tab marker that anchors text on the left with text expanding to the right.

**Tab-Right indent** A tab marker that anchors text on the right with text expanding to the left.

**Tab setting** A marker indicating the location to which a Tab code will move the cursor or place text that has been tabbed.

**Text** Readable characters including the alphanumeric characters, the numerals, and punctuation marks (Opposed to nonvisible control codes). Also, the words in a message.

**Toggle** The process of switching between two states. Also, any device, command, or command switch that has two states, on and off.

**Typeface** See Font.

**Type size** The (point) size of a printed character.

**Typeover mode** See Overwrite mode.

U

**Underlining** Paired codes that place a line beneath enclosed text.

**Unformatted disk** An uninitialized disk. The condition of the disk when first shipped.

**Unit of measurement** The scale by which characters are displayed and printed. The scale can be in inches, centimeters, point size, WordPerfect 4.2 column size, and other sizes.

**User interface** The manner in which a computer user accesses a software package's commands and files.

W

**Warm boot** Restarting the computer by pressing the Control, Alternate, and Delete keys instead of turning the computer off and then turning it back on.

**Wild cards** Characters used in DOS and WordPerfect commands and in search operations to match one or more characters in the position of the wild card in the string. A question mark matches one character, and an asterisk matches any number of characters.

**Window** A partial view of a larger document, worksheet, or database.

**Word wrap** The placement of a soft return code at the end of a line and the movement of a word outside of the hyphenation zone to the next line.

**WYSIWYG** (What you see is what you get) A word processor prints a document in a form identical to that seen on the monitor screen.

# INDEX